Leading by Example

A Journey of Business, Philanthropy, and Service

Ope Adeleke

Table of Contents

Preface

It is December 5th, 2017. New York City has been in the grip of a chilly frost over the last few weeks, but it is unseasonably mild today. Pewter gray clouds hang low in the sky, creating a blanket of warmth that envelops the streets of Manhattan and takes unsuspecting workers—clad sensibly for the winter in thick down jackets, hats, scarves, and gloves—by surprise during the morning commute when they emerge from subway stations or taxis. Traffic, as usual, crawls at a snail's pace along the wide boulevards and the bridges over the Hudson River, the exhaust fumes adding to the thickness of the atmosphere.

In the late afternoon, darkness arrives early, thanks in part to the low-hanging clouds. The humidity in Manhattan's streets reaches its peak. And then, the downpour begins.

The city is gearing up for the festive season, and colorful lights and decorations are strung between buildings, glowing brightly through the torrential sheets of rain. Shop windows show off elaborate Christmas displays, and visitors stop and study them, despite the inclement weather.

South of the shopping sector, right on the tip of the island of Manhattan, lies the Financial District. Centered around the infamous Wall Street, this is one of the most important financial areas in the world. Even in the bracing rain, there are tourists here too, wandering between the sky-high buildings, hoping for a glimpse of the rich, famous, and powerful; they leave the Stock Exchange or Federal Reserve Bank as evening arrives or pose for photographs alongside the

Charging Bull sculpture in the waning light. The bull is said to be a metaphor for the financial optimism and prosperity that this bustling area of the city exudes, and they are eager to capture it as a memento of their trip.

Cipriani Wall Street is another iconic sight in these parts. Previously home to the New York Merchants' Exchange, the United States Custom House, and the National City Bank's headquarters, this landmark building is now a prestigious restaurant and events venue. Inside the softly lit ballroom, the drum of the rain, the bustle of the tourists, and the inevitable growl of the traffic all disappear. Servers clad in starched white uniforms carefully lay cutlery—polished to a mirror-like sheen—and china in each place setting at the tables. Others bustle around straightening vases of fresh flowers or brushing at imaginary specks of dust, readying the venue for the evening's prestigious event. In another hour, the ballroom will play host to the Dwight D. Eisenhower Global Awards Gala. Presented by the Business Council for International Understanding (BICU), the award ceremony will attract distinguished businesspeople, entrepreneurs, philanthropists, and dignitaries from around the globe.

Outside, it is fully dark now, and the curtain of rain has yet to lift. Taxis, limos, and luxury cars, their windscreen wipers swishing frantically, make their way along Wall Street toward Cipriani, eliciting excited gasps from any tourists who are still braving the weather as they huddle beneath their umbrellas. One by one, they pull up to the grand colonnade at the entrance, and doormen in dark suits leap forward to open the vehicles' doors in an attempt to shield the eminent guests from some of the rain's force.

There are murmurs from the spontaneously assembled crowd as they attempt to recognize some of the guests who emerge in tuxedos and evening gowns, heads ducked against the weather. Cameras and phones are pointed at the entranceway, ready to capture a picture when they do. The excitement reaches its peak when former U.S. president George W. Bush—a notable supporter and friend to Africa, particularly because of his instrumental role in launching the landmark President's Emergency Plan for AIDS Relief (PEPFAR) initiative, the largest commitment of any nation in history to tackle a single disease—pauses to smile and wave at them, raindrops landing on his thick gray hair and the shoulders of his suit, before making his way inside.

It is a stunning setting: Cipriani has a towering 70-foot ceiling, vast marble floors, monolithic columns, and views across the Financial District. All in all, the opulence and luxury make the ideal backdrop for such an inspiring event. Each year, the nonprofit association, the BICU, holds this award ceremony to recognize the outstanding work of individuals in leadership, innovation, entrepreneurship, and citizenship. They aim to show the power that partnerships and strong international relationships can have in promoting understanding and success.

The awards are named after another former American President, Dwight D. Eisenhower. Though he never worked in the business sector himself—having achieved the highest rank at the Oval Office after a successful military career during World War Two—his leadership methods and strategies are still lauded by businesses and company leaders for their understated effectiveness. Eisenhower was a prestigious general before his tenure as U.S. President, leading both the Allied Forces' invasion of North Africa in 1942 and the D-Day Landings, where he was the Supreme Commander of the American soldiers and allied troops of over 12 nations that liberated Europe from Nazi control. He was one of only a handful of individuals to have achieved the rank of "Five-Star" General during his lifetime, marking him as one of the world's most senior military commanders. This is exactly why the BICU chose to celebrate innovators and entrepreneurs in his name: to draw attention to the way these individuals are trying to quietly and creatively solve some of the most important challenges around the world through economic development.

This year, once all of the delicious courses have been served by the efficient waiters and the guests have raised their glasses in a toast to most of the award winners, a historic moment takes place. The hosts for the gala, Kip Forbes (vice chairman of the Forbes Publishing empire) and Eisenhower's granddaughter, Annie, get ready to name the final winners of the evening.

"It is with great pleasure," Annie says, speaking softly but clearly into the microphone so that the hum of the dinner guests dies quickly away, "that I announce the first person to win this year's Global Entrepreneurship Award. He is known for his boldness and determination in business: exemplary characteristics of a visionary entrepreneur. He coined the term 'Africapitalism' and has been instrumental in demonstrating how private companies can be a powerful force in bringing about economic and social change in Africa. He is an advocate for bringing business, philanthropy, and social wealth together, and his can-do mindset in all areas is to be commended. Please welcome Anthony Onyemaechi Elumelu to the stage!"

There is great applause across the grand ballroom as this name is called. At a table on the right-hand side, Tony Elumelu rises to accept the award, making his way between the diners, accepting handshakes and congratulations as he approaches. Despite his humble beginnings and early financial hardship, he exudes confidence, even on such an opulent stage and among so many other eminent guests. He cuts an imposing figure in his smart tailored suit, crisp linen shirt, and trademark red tie. As he accepts the award graciously from Annie Eisenhower and Kip Forbes, his smile is broad and genuine. There are flashes below as photographers and journalists capture it. He turns to address the ballroom, and a hush falls over the gala once more.

"Thank you," Tony begins, "for this honor and your esteemed presence this evening. This is wonderful and symbolic for so many reasons." He smiles at his audience, with a small nod of recognition directed at both the BICU's leader and George W. Bush himself. It is a significant moment for Tony, but also for the international community as a whole: He is the first African to receive this award, and he knows that this will mean so much to many people.

"Eisenhower," Tony continues, "was a man who understood the importance of leadership. Being recognized today by an award in his name will resonate with so many people in Africa. We have a lot of enterprising and entrepreneurial brains on the African continent; what they need is purposeful leadership. This award further energizes, encourages, and motivates me to do even more to support young, enterprising Africans who seek opportunities.

"I also hope that this recognition will inspire other Africans and friends of Africa who want to give and support us in a manner that helps empower our young ones, encourage our women, and makes sure that we can work together for an inclusive prosperity—one that touches everyone almost evenly."

As he thinks of the hundreds of young people that he has already helped through the work of his foundation and those that could possibly benefit in the future as a result of the publicity and respect that this award will bring, Tony's smile widens further. For a moment, however, it all feels rather unreal: the sea of eminent guests looking up from around the circular tables, the crystal glasses of expensive wine raised up in recognition of his achievements and ideology, the impeccable cut of his own tailored suit. The mix of candlelight and historic chandeliers gives everything in the room an otherworldly glow, almost as if it exists only in a dream.

He has a momentary flashback to himself as a young boy, writing his homework at a scarred wooden desk in the window of his family home, head bent close to the paper in order to see the letters clearly in the low light of a kerosene lamp. As he glances around the room, Tony feels a wave of emotion at just how far he has come while following his head, heart, and dreams. There is another camera flash, and Tony wonders if that picture will make it into newspapers or onto the global news the next morning. He hopes that it has captured the depth of his passion and achievement in his eyes. Perhaps, it will inspire another young boy or girl, sitting with their homework, somewhere very far away from the opulence of this ballroom and far away from the prosperity of Manhattan, to embark upon their own journeys to success.

"I must also," Tony continues, clearing his throat, "take a moment to mention my wonderful wife." He goes on to dedicate the award to his family, his mentors, and the staff at his investment group, Heirs Holdings, thanking those who have supported him during his decades working in finance and business. He has always been a man to place a premium value on the close relationships he holds with his family and loyal associates and colleagues. "They have made not only my own success possible, but they have also been instrumental in helping thousands of young Africans achieve their dreams through the Tony

Elumelu Foundation. I hope that this is just the beginning of the prosperity of Africa."

Tony raises his hand to the crowd in a gesture of thanks, and applause accompanies him back to his chair.

Afterward, when the second winner of the award has been announced and all the china and glasses cleared away by the indefatigable waiters, the guests take their leave of one another, preparing to head back to their homes or hotels through the stormy night. Tony accepts the praise and congratulations of his peers as he shares the vision he has for his charitable foundation and the commitments he has made to its future. His eyes shine. The smile does leave his face for the rest of the evening. Such is his talent, commitment, and drive that Tony has received many other accolades. But this recognition—one that takes place on a prominent, global stage, named for a leader who was famed for the example he provided and who believed strongly in promoting international understanding—is something that he has strived for. It is what he has envisaged for Africa as a whole and for the many individuals whom he has supported through his philanthropic work.

When he looks back at the rain-lashed facade of Cipriani as his taxi pulls away, he experiences a deep sense of satisfaction and pride. Tomorrow, he will carry on working toward a better future for Africa, but tonight, he can take a moment to bask in the glory of the award he has received.

Tony's story is one of perseverance, determination, and a deep belief in the power of hard work and innovation to create lasting change.

This book will tell his inspiring story and share the lessons he learned along the course of his journey to success. It is also a story of the challenges he faced, in both his personal life and business endeavors, and how he overcame these potential obstacles. Within these pages, you will learn of the significant moments which occurred in his life and career, from his early days in Nigeria to his work on the global stage and his award-winning efforts to bring prosperity to his home continent. Together, we will reflect on the lessons he learned along this journey of business, philanthropy, and service, offering insights into his philosophy and his vision for the future of entrepreneurship in Africa.

In many ways, his life is a roadmap for others who wish to follow in his path.

Above all, this book is a testament to the power of one individual to make a difference in the world. It is a story of hope, resilience, and the boundless potential of human ingenuity. Tony Elumelu has always led by example; my belief is that this book will inspire others to pursue their dreams, no matter how difficult or daunting they may seem. I hope that it will encourage you to think about how you can be part of the future and have a positive impact on the world around you. I hope that it helps us build a better world for us all.

Thank you for taking the time to read Tony's story.

Chapter 1:

Humble Beginnings

Jos, Nigeria, 1963

First, let us go back to the beginning of Tony's journey: to Jos, in northern central Nigeria and the humble beginnings of our story.

Nigeria is the most populous country in Africa and has been nicknamed the "Giant of Africa" for its vast geographical area as well as its large population. Located in the west of the continent, it is also characterized by the diversity of its people, culture, and landscapes, which range variously from plains to deserts to jungles across this huge space. Nigeria is also the most prosperous and powerful of the West African nations and wields considerable international influence, despite the poverty which still afflicts many of its citizens and its troubled political history.

Jos lies more than 250 kilometers northeast of the capital city, Abuja, in the north-central Plateau State. Around this hill town, vast swathes of open grassland stretch to a horizon that is outlined by the taller peaks of the state's eponymous plateau. Shere Hills—the remarkable rocky outcrop that overlooks the town—forms one of the highest points in Nigeria. Thanks to such a high elevation, Jos enjoys one of the coolest climates in the country. Diverse flora and fauna flourish in these conditions.

Once, long ago, much of the area was woodland. However, the encroachment of grazing and farming onto this natural landscape over the centuries means that there are now only occasional clumps of cacti and scattered trees as far as the eye can see, though some wooded valleys remain in the south of the state around the Benue River. The fast-flowing water forms a natural boundary along its banks. There are surprising moments of ancient beauty still visible here, with rushing waterfalls and deep pools formed among the trees, away from the rolling plains which have been transformed by the need for agricultural land.

The original settlement at Jos was a small farming village of the Birom people—a place where the inhabitants eked out a living on the grasslands, with their herds and crops providing a certain level of self-sufficiency. For many generations, the local people were simply occupied by growing the grains acha and millet, as well as staples such as yams, maize, potatoes, and rice. Alongside these crops, Fulani herdsmen allowed their cattle to graze along the elevated plains.

It was in these fields and streams, and around these stunning rock formations, that Tony Elumelu spent much of his time as a child, exploring the hills and valleys around Jos, playing with his siblings and friends, and dreaming of what the future might hold for an ambitious young boy. Today, despite its checkered past, the natural beauty, unique scenery, and temperate climates draw in their share of tourists.

When colonial rule officially began in 1884, this small agricultural settlement was transformed into one of the first major cities in Nigeria. At first, the British simply brought much-needed construction works and transportation links with them. Then, at the turn of the 20th century, an irreversible change to the community, landscape, and economy occurred here: In 1903, the British colonizers learned of the tin deposits in the area. They began mining the metal on an industrial scale. The locals had long since gathered small amounts of it from the beds of the streams across the plateau; the British, however, wanted to extract as much as they possibly could from the riches that the ground held, without much thought or consideration for the Plateau State's agricultural history or economic future.

As a result, Jos saw a huge period of development over the next half a century, with more railway lines opened so that the valuable tin deposits could be easily exported, and housing and infrastructure were built up quickly to house the commercial enterprise and its workers. The growth in the area was fast, but the majority of the money and prosperity that came in its wake was sent abroad along with the mined resources. The local community did not really benefit from either the creation of wealth or investment—a situation that was repeated time and again in far too many other parts of Africa as a result of colonialism.

This rapid rise of this industry—particularly during the Second World War, when the output of the mines became even more valuable to the British—also brought many outsiders to the site. This had always been an area that was known for its rich cultural heritage and diverse population, with the state being home to more than 40 ethnic groups, but the lure of jobs and prosperity created an even more diverse meeting point of cultures and tribes. Among the groups who traveled here were a number of Igbo people from the southeastern regions of Nigeria. Among them were Suzanne and Dominic Elumelu: Tony's parents.

In 1963, when Tony was born, there were a number of smelteries constructed near Jos, and the country's economy was strongly reliant on the mining that occurred in the area at that time. However, by the end of the 1960s, after Nigeria gained its independence and endured the long period of violence and unrest that ensued, this had all changed again. When peace was achieved once more, the petroleum industry in the south of the country became the dominant economic force in Nigeria instead. Although some local enterprise continued, much of the boom of prosperity surrounding the mines eroded, and Jos was no longer an important center of commerce. Without many other opportunities to pursue elsewhere, the inhabitants of Jos stayed in the area, even without their jobs at the mines, and so, the city continued to grow and become the largest in the region, despite being afflicted by poverty. In 1975, it became the administrative capital of the Plateau State during a reorganization of some of the state boundaries, but this did not change the fact that life continued to be hard for its residents on a day-to-day basis.

In his formative years, Tony witnessed the challenges that this change in economic circumstances and the awful civil war during the 1960s had on the people in the community around him. Many of his friends, classmates, and neighbors struggled to make ends meet. Many found it hard to access quality education. Despite their work ethic, many lacked the opportunities and tools to build a better life for themselves and their families. Unemployment and poverty were rife, and there was little investment or economic intervention from the central government to try to tackle it. It was seeing such challenges firsthand as a child that fueled much of Tony's determination to make a difference—not only for himself but also for those around him.

While there has been some urban development around the old center of the city in more recent years, Jos has not seen as much change as other cities and towns in Nigeria. This is partly because it was one of the first cities built by the British during colonial rule: Most of its structure and sites retain this old-fashioned feel today, and thus, Jos is harder to transform than cities that don't have this heritage at their core. As a result of its colonial importance and the breathtaking countryside which surrounds it, however, Jos has remained a popular tourist destination. Despite all of the hardship here, it is a place of great beauty—and great potential. It is a place that could, through Tony's vision of the future of Africa, be transformed into a thriving, prosperous city.

Tony is not the only prominent figure to have called the cosmopolitan city of Jos home, nor is he alone in believing in its potential. Jos is the birthplace of several politicians and heads of state, including Solomon Lar, the first civilian governor of Plateau State, and former military leaders Murtala Ramat Mohammed and Yakubu Gowon. Nollywood actor Desmond Elliott, footballers Patrick Olusegun Odegbami and Ahmed Musa also grew up there, along with rapper Panshak Henry Zamani, whose song *Oleku* is one of the most sampled and remixed tunes of all time in Nigeria.

Tony still visits when he can, although it is many miles—and worlds away in other respects as well—from his current home in Lagos. And when he reflects on his place of birth, Tony sees how integral the town of Jos was to the start of his journey and career. It is a place that has shaped his life in many ways, a place that will hold a special significance in his heart, not just as the city where he was born but as the place which first sparked his dreams of what he might come to achieve in the future. It was there, surrounded by struggle, that he could see the value of hard work, determination, and leadership for local communities.

Family and Childhood

Suzanne and Dominic Elumelu were hardworking, honest people who believed in traditional values and a strong work ethic. They left behind the Igbo community and their home in Aniocha North to seek prosperity in Jos during a time when many others also arrived in the area. They had five children together, and they encouraged them all to think creatively when it came to money and success—just as they had done when they traveled across their homeland in search of new horizons.

When Tony was a child, his parents were both entrepreneurs in their own right. Suzanne, in particular, enjoyed the advantage of the Igbo culture's encouragement of women to be influential outside the home. She worked hard to break out of the constraints of the domestic role typically assigned to women in the patriarchal society of Nigeria (and much of the rest of the world) at the time. She worked in the restaurant sector, leading and managing businesses with the force of her determination, passion, and confidence. Dominic was also a businessman. Between them, they created an atmosphere at home in which Tony's natural ability and innate ambition could thrive—even when the opportunities in the town that they had relocated to began to dwindle.

From an early age, Tony knew that he wanted to do something big with his life. He was driven by the same desire to succeed as his parents and was keen to both make his family proud and help others. He would listen to his parents talk animatedly at the dinner table about the successes or struggles of their day, absorbing their energy and reflectiveness as they spoke. He admired the way that they set out for work, each time determined, no matter what had happened at work or in the town the day before that might make their jobs that little bit harder. They were strong role models for him in all aspects, and he saw how important the qualities of resilience and strength were to succeeding in a community that was often battered by the political turmoil of the fledgling independent nation of Nigeria.

As one of five siblings, Tony was surrounded by noise, warmth, and friendship at home, no matter the economic hardship or unrest which swirled around their family unit. They were all very close as children: They spent a lot of time together, playing games, exploring the countryside, and supporting one another through the ups and downs of daily life. His siblings were his best friends and closest confidants, and they remain close to this day, despite the different directions in which adulthood took them. They were bound together, in many ways, by their parents' belief in a bright future for Africa, as a whole, and their children, in particular—the same belief which had led them to move to Jos and away from their friends and relatives.

However, in 1967, when Tony had only just begun to attend the local school, the simmering unease and waning prosperity of the Plateau State was dramatically escalated by civil war. Only a few short years after achieving independence from the British, Nigeria was plunged into chaos.

The arrival of the British colonizers in the region during the late 19th century was a catalyst that changed the relationship between the many diverse ethnic groups in Nigeria. The Igbo people—who had mostly lived in self-contained communities without hierarchy or the need for much interaction with neighboring tribes—began, increasingly, to come into contact with other groups as the country was altered under the increasing influence of British rule. While the divisions between some of the major cultural groups dissipated as a result of this social shift—setting aside differences to band together against their colonizers—the opposite was true for the Igbo people. Instead, they started to develop a more pronounced sense of their own ethnic identity, in contrast to other groups of Nigeria. This caused them to feel distinct and separate from the rest of the population at a time when some other societal barriers were being eroded. As a result, the Igbo became more and more isolated.

After the initial proclamation of independence in October 1960, Nigeria became a republic in 1963, the year of Tony's birth. But when the new federal government failed to provide the stability, development, and creation of wealth that many communities had hoped for and the nascent republic slipped further into economic and social decline, the next few years were marked by increasing tension and dissatisfaction. As the new federal government attempted to combine the many diverse people and groups living in Nigeria, rather than recognizing and respecting the distinctions between them, they fanned the flames of rebellion that had already been brewing in certain communities. This caused tensions to mount further, and in 1967, there was a bloody coup d'etat in the Northern region which came at a terrible price: civil war, military rule, and the murder of many Igbo civilians.

In response, the Igbo people tried, in turn, to claim the Eastern region as an independent homeland and protect themselves from the shadow of threats and violence they faced in the rest of the nation. This area became known as Biafra, and the appalling hardships and suffering that ensued became the Biafran War. For the next three years, the Igbo people in Biafra were blighted by malnutrition, famine, and genocide as the federal army refused to cede control of the area. Eventually, ravaged by these horrors, the temporary Igbo government had no choice but to surrender to Nigerian rule in 1970.

Luckily for Tony, he was too young to experience much of this awfulness firsthand, although his parents and community were not exempt from the horror. All Tony can remember is that, one day, when he was just four years old, he was told not to go to the school where he had only just become a pupil or to play outside with his friends. His parents had not gone to work that morning, which was a highly unusual break in their routine, nor had his older siblings gone to their schools. He was too young to understand the political machinations and coups which resulted from the nation's tensions. At the time, he knew only the stability of his childhood home and supportive family. He knew only that many of his friends spoke different languages and had different religions; he could not understand the consequences of such diversity when violence erupted. He did not understand that Igbo people, like him and his family, were the targets of this violence. Instead, he knew only that he was disappointed to be kept indoors, away from his usual habits and games. Nigerian children were not encouraged to ask questions of the adults, so Tony and his siblings did not confront their parents about their confusion. But they overheard enough of the whisperings and anxieties around the house to know that the situation was dire—particularly for their own Igbo family.

Outside the relative safety of their home, the streets were filled with commotion, loud noises, and shouting that day. They were forced to wait in their home on tenterhooks as the civil war began to rage around them.

It came as a brutal shock to the inhabitants of Jos and the Plateau State: This had always been a peaceful area. For centuries, they had lived side-by-side with their neighbors from differing tribes. They were used to living in harmony, despite the fact that over 200 different languages and dialects were spoken on the Plateau. Schools were places of diversity, where children learned their friends' words for everyday objects or used Hausa as a common language between them. The looting of Igbo houses and businesses and the killing of innocent people was, therefore, beyond distressing for the majority of the residents. And yet, enthralled by the violence and unrest occurring in other parts of the country, some carried out these atrocities on their neighbors, even in peaceful Jos.

After the dust from those first extreme days of fighting had settled, Suzanne and Dominic tried to shield their children from the worst of the tension that continued to blight Nigeria. As Igbo people, they were in a precarious position during the years of the civil war, despite the distance of Jos from the independent state of Biafra and the inherent peacefulness of their community. They were not caught up in the starvation and oppression of Igboland in the Republic of Biafra, but they were still discriminated against by the federal government. They were denied access to their savings from before the war and often had trouble finding employment as a result of the prejudices against them by other groups and the non-Igbo government. As a result, the Igbo became the poorest citizens of Nigeria. It took many decades for Igbo individuals to regain some status and positions of authority, thus overturning the discrimination and hardships that they had faced during the period and aftermath of military rule.

However, Igbo culture is characterized by creativity, an adventurous spirit, and respect for divine powers, and Tony's family were great examples of this sense of faith and resilience in the face of adversity. They knew that they were lucky to escape the violence that ravaged their nation; this further fuelled their determination to work hard and help their children avoid such experiences in adulthood.

So, despite everything that happened in Nigeria during his early childhood, Tony was fortunate to have such a supportive family—one who encouraged him to pursue his dreams and reach for the stars. Tony's parents may not have been wealthy during his formative years, but they saw the value of education and knew that it could become a way to open doors and create opportunities for their children. They did everything they could to help him get ahead through academic means, including enrolling him in school as early as they could and providing him with the resources that he needed to succeed in lessons, even if it was a financial struggle to do so. Tony's parents made many sacrifices to ensure that all of their five children could attend school, and their selflessness gave the Elumelu siblings a deep appreciation for learning from a young age.

As soon as it was safe to do so in 1967, Tony and his brothers and sisters eagerly returned to school to continue their studies. Even when times were incredibly hard, Tony's parents did not lose sight of the value of education or the importance of studying, and they encouraged the children to read or complete academic exercises whilst they waited out the result of the military coup. They were determined for their children to succeed, despite the challenges of their own financial situation and the instability which swirled around the little oasis of calm, kindness, and diligence that they had created for their family.

Day after day, tired from their own work, Tony's parents would nevertheless spend long evenings supporting Tony and his siblings in their studies. Tony can still recall the many nights he spent learning by the light of a kerosene lamp, motivated by words of encouragement and his parents' belief in the doors that his education could one day open for him. It is an inspiring image: a young boy, motivated only by his family and his inner drive, studying in the midst of poverty and war, in a place and time where many other individuals may simply have given up. But he never lost sight of his goals or his parents' love.

Overall, despite the difficulties that he faced, Tony's childhood was shaped by the love and support of his family and his determination to attend school and make friends within the community against this backdrop. His parents, who had come from humble beginnings themselves, worked hard and spent long hours improving their businesses in order to overcome the limitations placed on Igbo people during the 1960s and '70s. Watching them toil and listening to them talk about the importance of making your own way in the world instilled a sense of discipline, respect, and determination in Tony and his siblings. He valued the example they set for him, especially in the face of economic hardships and discrimination—circumstances he only truly came to understand when he was much older and which only served to further deepen his admiration for his parents and what they helped him achieve during his own childhood.

Tony's family has been the foundation of his success, providing him with the tools he needed to achieve his goals and make a difference in the world. He is grateful for the lessons he learned during his childhood and the memories he shares with his parents and siblings, who have been there for him from the beginning and who stood by his side, encouraging him through some of Nigeria's darkest hours.

Education

Nigeria's structured school system began under the British model, partly because it was European Christian missionaries that first established formalized education there. After independence, both the republic and military governments which followed continued to follow the same system—although, it has since been reformed to shadow the American style of education in more recent years.

Initially, before Nigeria was brought under British control, education took place in Islamic and Indigenous schools which limited children's schooling to the Quran and local customs respectively. However, after several decades of the formal system created during colonial rule, Tony's education in the 1960s consisted of attendance at a primary school for the first six years, beginning from age four.

Although the facilities and availability of school places varied widely from region to region across such a large country, the majority of young children were encouraged to attend school where possible during this period. Attendance was still sporadic, as it had been since the initial introduction of formal education by the missionaries, but more and more communities and families were beginning to see its importance for future growth, just like the Elumelus. Similarly, many academics and officials during this period following independence campaigned to make the government recognize education as an important part of Nigeria's growth as a democratic republic and more widely encourage its citizens to see how learning could play a key role in driving prosperity and contributing to nation-building. Despite the challenges of creating a single unified system across such a vast area and diverse population, along with issues of funding across the sector,

Nigeria nevertheless soon became a leader in West Africa in terms of educational policy. School attendance and literacy levels grew faster in Nigeria than throughout many of its neighbors, and these remain at higher levels than in many other African countries.

Like his siblings and many of his neighbors, Tony began his education at a local primary school in Jos that was typical of both the time and the region. These small schools were attended by children from diverse backgrounds and ethnic groups—reflecting the cultural melting pot of the community in Jos and the Plateau State as a whole—and they often communicated with each other in either Igbo or Hausa, the more widely spoken languages, in a multilingual context. However, because of the range of dialects spoken and as a result of lingering colonial influence, English tended to be the language used by educators across the curriculum.

At his primary school, Tony was instructed in reading and writing—in both English and the major languages of Nigeria—as well as mathematics, religious knowledge, agricultural science, and home economics. He was an exemplary student: curious, determined, and respectful. Despite the nationwide tension and upheaval swirling around his family and local community, Tony faithfully attended school as regularly as possible. His parents had already instilled in him a deep appreciation for education and the possibilities that it could open up for him at home, and his first experiences of school in Jos helped him to further develop this love of learning and passion for discovery. Right from the start of his school career, he loved to listen to the teachers impart their knowledge and to practice the skills he had been taught in class when at home. He would sit, diligently and attentively, at his rickety desk in the drafty room, hands clasped together on its surface. Once he had learned to form his letters, he would write down as many of his teachers' words as he could, in addition to repeating the answers verbally with the rest of the class; his pencil was always poised and ready. It could be hot and overcrowded in the school at times, especially during the summer months, but Tony did not waver from his commitment to getting the most out of the lessons he knew he was lucky to have the opportunity to enjoy. From a very early age, he also showed a keen, analytical mind. He was often thinking above and beyond the situation or problem-solving required of a lesson or homework task.

Despite basic education at primary level being both free and compulsory for children in Nigeria once formalized schooling was established, not all children attended school or had the benefit of parents who pushed for them to succeed in the face of hardship. In the difficult years following their proclamation of independence, in which Nigeria sought —and ultimately failed—to learn the ropes of democracy and faced the crisis of a civil war, the country's infrastructure inevitably suffered. Electricity and power were often unreliable. School funding could be infrequent and resources inadequate. The facilities and buildings were typically poorly maintained. Teachers sometimes even left without warning in the middle of the year, disrupting the continuance of the students' learning.

Yet, whilst attendance statistics dipped lower than usual during these years across the country, Tony did not allow such challenges to affect his educational journey. He carried his belief in the importance of education with him through the financial struggles faced by both his parents and the local community and the disruption of power supplies, missing textbooks, absent teachers, and rain dripping through the dilapidated roof during lessons. He was determined to achieve his goals and pursue his dreams even when, during primary school, he did not yet have a clear vision of what those goals and dreams might be. All he knew at the time—encouraged by both his teachers' talk of building a strong Republic of Nigeria in the future and by his parents' work ethic—was that he wanted to somehow work in business. Like many young, eager Nigerians at the time, he saw business as a key to success, although it was a number of years before he understood the intricacies behind this dream.

Tony idolized his uncle (his mother's brother) who visited them sporadically, clad in smart Western-inspired clothes and polished shoes. His parents would tell him and his siblings rather grandly, albeit vaguely, that his uncle was a businessman. The work or job itself was never discussed in more specific terms, and so, this became something to imagine and visualize—a role much more glamorous than his mother or father's work, the struggles and daily grind of which he was very familiar with. Instead, Tony pictured the life of a businessman to be an alluring fantasy of success, without specifics—but that was what made it so appealing. Whenever his charismatic uncle came to visit, it added fuel to the fire of Tony's dream to one day walk in this world.

Tony graduated from primary school at the age of 11; many of his friends and neighbors in Jos, however, did not continue to study after this basic, compulsory part of their education had been completed. Some continued to attend primary school for more than the standard six years, until they had reached the desired standard in assessment, but most simply left the school system before their teenage years. Across the country as a whole, the percentage of the community attending secondary education was much lower than those in primary school, partly as a result of the continued political instability and social unrest and partly due to poverty. Many families encouraged their children into their workforce at the age of 11, desperately needing their help to provide the household with some income if they could find a job. Others who could not source employment were encouraged to leave education to complete more domestic chores or help raise younger siblings. For both Tony and his parents, however, there was never any doubt that he would attend the next level of his education. He was one of a small number of children in Jos whose family was prepared to put every resource and penny they had into allowing them to continue to study beyond the primary level.

Secondary school also followed the British model, with five years of education to achieve a General Certificate in Education, then a final two years to complete A-Level exams. Here, Tony was introduced to a wider range of subjects, including science, civic studies, business, and entrepreneurship. He continued to excel academically. He was always a diligent student, eager to learn and explore new ideas, and he again embraced the knowledge imparted by the teachers, relishing the chance to explore these new topics and ideas.

Although the civil war had ended, the continuation of military rule in the 1970s meant that funding for Nigerian schools and the development of a consistent national educational policy was not always a priority. The building and facilities at Tony's secondary school were little better than those of the primary one in town, but this did not distract him from his determination to achieve strong grades in his assessments.

Time and again, after sitting down to a traditional Igbo family meal—such as *Utara na ofe*, or "swallow and soup," consisting of a starch such as yams or rice alongside a soup or stew—Tony would read or study well into the evening hours. He was popular and had plenty of friends, in addition to his close relationships with his siblings, but he was also dedicated and determined, to the extent that his studies often took priority over hobbies or social engagements. He carried this innate drive to succeed throughout his school career, and he was rewarded with the good results he had dreamed of at the end of seven further years of academic diligence.

However, after finishing secondary school, Tony was faced with a critical decision about what to do next. Despite his academic achievements in his A-Levels and the sacrifices his family had made to help him through secondary school, they were not able to afford to provide the same level of support in order to help to send him to university. Ultimately, it came down to the additional costs involved. He was thus faced with the prospect of leaving education behind and entering the workforce at a young age, like so many of his peers and neighbors had been forced to do.

Whilst Tony was confident he could build a decent career for himself from this point, both he and his parents believed that a university education could open more doors in the long run. Nigeria had been one of the first African nations to invest in a tertiary education system, with the first university established in 1948 during colonial rule and further education study becoming increasingly popular in the years following independence. The establishment of a university provided young Nigerians with advanced learning in various fields of study, which both the new republic and the British before them understood to be paramount to the continued development and advancement of Nigeria's economy through the power of a skilled workforce.

To thus encourage the growth of skilled labor and employment, two more institutions were created by the new government soon after independence, with a larger wave of second- and third-generation universities further established after 1975. However, it was still a small, emerging sector when Tony left secondary school, with adequate investment remaining elusive, just as it had in the primary and secondary education tiers. Nigeria's large population and youthful demographic also ensured that there was far more demand for places than availability at these new institutions. As a result, university study was still seen as the domain of the privileged and wealthy in the 1970s and '80s, rather than as a right, like a compulsory primary school education.

Another reason that university was inaccessible to many young Nigerians, including Tony, was also due to the fact that, despite the government's commitment to keeping undergraduate degrees free, students were compelled to pay for their meal tickets and accommodation during their studies, which essentially amounted to paying fees.

A rise in these prices announced by the government in 1978 had made university even less affordable for many prospective and current students. This change, coupled with the frustration that many young people felt about the low numbers of university places, led to violent demonstrations and riots in April of that year. These became known as the "Ali Must Go" protests after the Minister for Education at the time, Ahmadu Ali. Hoping to reverse the government's decision about the increase in fees and draw attention to the importance of the voice of students in politics, they at first boycotted lectures and then, when the government refused to listen, took to the streets. They clashed publicly with the police and military, and several students were killed. Universities were forced to close, and civil unrest spread across the country as a result. Despite their protests, however, the increase in fees remained.

Yet, the widespread chaos which resulted was not without effect: It legitimized the power of the nascent student movement and provided an important foundation for union action in the future. It demonstrated how willing students were to protest their rights and make themselves heard and showed the role that educated young citizens wanted to play in the creation of a strong, prosperous Nigeria. After these protests, they became a pressure group that the military government had no choice but to recognize as important.

By the beginning of the 1980s, when Tony had turned 18 and was ready to consider enrolling in further education, this unrest had been somewhat resolved within the students' ranks. However, the desire to attend university continued to be increasingly prevalent among ambitious young Nigerians, and demand still outstripped the capacity at the available institutions. The increased fees for meals and accommodation also had to be considered; this was why Tony's family were unable to financially support him beyond secondary school, during which he was able to live and eat at home. As Tony's educational ambitions would require him to leave home, he would have to pay the stipend for accommodation and meals during his three years of undergraduate study. It was a sum that remained out of reach.

But Tony was determined not to let financial obstacles stand in his way. He continued his education by enrolling in evening classes and working simultaneously as a furniture salesman during the day, saving every penny he could, and hoping to put it towards a university education in the future. It was a difficult and tiring time, but Tony remained committed to his goal. Eventually, Tony's hard work paid off. He was able to save up enough money for the initial payments needed and, thus, was able to make an application to a university.

Thanks to his strong high school grades, he was quickly accepted into Bendel State University (now known as Ambrose Alli University), which had been newly established in 1981 as part of the government's attempts to increase the capacity of tertiary education in Nigeria following the protests. Even with the creation of new schools, however, there were thousands of applications for only hundreds of places. Tony was grateful to have the chance to further his academic pursuits. He threw himself into his undergraduate studies, determined to make the most of this opportunity.

Early Ambitions and Outlook

Whilst he had the usual dreams of parties and friends during his time at university, Tony was always looking ahead to the future. He was aware, alongside his day-to-day concerns, that the journey to success was not linear. He had seen this firsthand during his own road to enrolment at university, which had not been as straightforward as some of his classmates'. For Tony, it had been about more than gaining the required grades from secondary school: He had had to make sacrifices and work hard in order to fund his admission to further education. He knew that he had to be determined and do everything that was needed to achieve success in the academic world because he saw this as an excellent long-term opportunity. From a young age, he could see the importance of thinking ahead and having a plan for the following 10 years of his education and career, when many of his peers thought only of the next day or week. This was one of the reasons why he chose to study economics; it was a subject that he believed would provide the strongest overall knowledge of employment and business and open up the most varied career paths to him in the world of work.

Throughout his undergraduate degree, he maintained his ironclad discipline. He never shied away from challenges because he understood that overcoming them could provide opportunities and that opportunities could lead to the success of his vision. However, he still did not expect to enter a life of entrepreneurship at this time, although his decision to study economics gave him the opportunity to learn much about the business world from a theoretical perspective. Economics was—and still is today—one of the most popular courses offered to and undertaken by students in Nigeria. Many young citizens, just like Tony, found that they had an impetus to understand the commercial and financial context in which they were operating, often in the hope that they would be able to both enjoy future success themselves and help their nation to overcome some of the obstacles hindering its development.

However, Tony's economic education did not just come from university. Further to his studies, one of the things that helped to give him an understanding of the practicalities of working and business was his mother. When he was 20 and at university, she owned a restaurant, and during his holidays, Tony would return home from his accommodation on campus to help her there. During the long hours working alongside Suzanne, Tony would often think about the intricacies of the business and how it worked, considering the balance between profit, loss, and the number of customers. Sometimes, he would imagine the restaurant operating on a larger scale, using his natural ability to problem solve and think critically to consider both the benefits and disadvantages of this model.

Similarly, whenever he read a newspaper or a magazine, he would wonder about the practicalities involved with a business within the area or topic that he was reading about. From fish ponds to bakeries, his mind was always active, considering the issues and costs of setting up one such enterprise, how he would manage or run it, or how he might be able to make a profit from it. He was, in these moments of reflection, growing his knowledge of commerce in a way that complemented the education he was receiving during this period. His mind was (often subconsciously) creating, tracking, and shaping ideas that helped him in his journey to entrepreneurship.

Despite his determined nature and ability to think ahead, Tony's early ambitions were relatively modest when compared to the success he has actually achieved during his lifetime. He did, at times, think vaguely that he might start a business himself one day. After all, he admired the way that his mother had built her way up to running her own restaurant, along with the glamor of his charismatic businessman uncle. Though he was often thinking about commerce alongside his daily activities, these were not the thoughts or ideas at the forefront of his mind during his youth. After his first semester at Bendel State University, his initial aim was to complete his Bachelor's degree in Economics to a high standard and then go on to study for a Master's in the same subject. This was because he hoped to start his career by working in a bank. It was a goal that was partly shaped by the images of successful men working in the banking sector in Nigeria during the 1980s that covered the newspapers and magazines Tony enjoyed reading at the time. They were power dressers, characterized by their suspenders, suits, and shiny brogue shoes. Tony was highly attracted by the outward shine of their success, as he had been to his uncle's. He wanted the whole outfit—and the lifestyle that went along with it.

Thanks to a period of relative economic growth and the injection of funds by a host of international investors, Nigeria's banks began to post huge profits during the 1980s. While much of the nation struggled to gain an even keel in other industries which were still beset by challenges of infrastructure and wildly fluctuating costs or prices, the financial sector actually benefited from the continued instability of the situation. They were able to post high returns on investment and grow their balance sheets as a result of the cycle of boom and bust in the businesses that banked with them. When these profits began to catch the attention of investors, this stimulated an interest in banking among students and graduates for its perceived profitability. During this decade, therefore, the number of banks and people working in the industry grew rapidly. The bankers and their suspenders thus became an iconic symbol of success at the time: an image that the ambitious young Tony Elumelu hoped to emulate once he had graduated himself. For Tony, and many other students of business and economics in Nigeria at the time, banking began to represent the path to opportunity which they craved.

It wasn't, however, a pathway that was without difficulty. Despite the advancement in the banking sector, most other aspects of the Nigerian economy were struggling. The government was often at the center of scandal, with rumors of bribes and corruption running rife. The civil war had ended in 1970 when the leaders of Biafra surrendered unconditionally, but the humanitarian crises caused by the years of conflict were far from resolved. Poverty and economic inequality were widespread. Unemployment levels were high, especially among the youth, and even for school and university graduates with good qualifications. All in all, it was not an environment that was conducive to financial prosperity, even with the determined spirit and ambitious nature of individuals like Tony Elumelu.

There was, however, some hope in the darkness: Having become the Nigerian Head of State at the young age of 31, General Gowon successfully led Nigeria through the tragedy of the Biafran War. His administration—composed of a relatively youthful cabinet, with ministers of a similar age—then undertook bold economic and infrastructural initiatives. Ultimately, this increased Nigeria's gross domestic product (GDP) and began to improve living standards through investment in agriculture, industry, and infrastructure, especially in terms of his administration's Second National Development Plan (1970–1974). Gowon was also responsible for launching Nigeria's Universal Primary Education (UPE) program in 1973, with the goal of providing free and compulsory primary education to all Nigerian children: a significant initiative and key milestone in Nigeria's educational development that continues to impact the nation to this day. Gowon's administration similarly invested in infrastructure, including roads, bridges, hospitals, and schools, with a focus on improving transportation networks and healthcare facilities. After Nigeria's difficult and divisive Biafran War, General Gowon (whose father had been a catechist with the Church Missionary Society in Northern Nigeria) personally promoted policies aimed at fostering national unity and reconciliation, including the famous "No Victor, No Vanquished" declaration.

Chapter 2:

Starting Out

National Youth Service Corps

In 1985, when Tony graduated from Bendel State University with his undergraduate degree in economics, he had dreams of continuing even further on his academic journey with a postgraduate degree. Intelligent and dedicated, he was an ideal candidate for further study in another of the new institutions which had been established since 1980 as part of the so-called "third-generation" universities. In order to match the economic and social demand, these institutions, like Bendel State, were being set up by individuals or academic committees in order to increase the availability of courses in relevant sectors such as technology and agriculture across the country. Because of the high levels of unemployment which still plagued Nigeria, the government was keen to support such ventures, hoping to create more skilled graduates who could enter the workforce and continue to push the country toward economic development. Federal investment in higher education at this time was thus increasing, and Tony sought to take advantage of this situation by pursuing another degree before he applied for jobs in finance.

However, before he embarked on a Masters' program, he had to complete the National Youth Service Corp (NYSC) which was—and still is, at the time of publication—compulsory for all Nigerians to undertake after their graduation from university. Established in 1973 by the military government that was in power at the time, the NYSC was first created as a strategy to begin the rebuilding of the nation after the devastation of the Biafran War and help to create a strong republic that was still in its infancy after independence over a decade before. There was no military conscription in Nigeria at the time, unlike in many other countries around the world, so the year of service for the NYSC was a way to engage young people in the government's vision for their nation's future. The scheme was aimed specifically at university graduates (below the age of 30) in order to ensure those with the best career opportunities and economic chances understood the government's goals and values. They were essentially required to work as volunteers for a year, undertaking unpaid experience for employers but provided with a small stipend by the government in order to pay for their living expenses. As Nigeria is still a developing nation and continues to face many socio-economic challenges, the scheme has been continued in an effort to overcome these issues, although there have been some calls in recent years to retire it.

The program was established not only to give graduates practical experience of industry and instill a strong work ethic in them—which was deemed essential for nation-building—but also to try to balance the ambitions of individuals with loyal, patriotic service. The government wanted their new, skilled members of the workforce to be committed to their objectives and to hold a sense of shared mission in creating a strong economy in Nigeria. It was hoped that this common mindset, alongside the increased investment in education, would accelerate the country's growth.

During their year of service, NYSC members were required to live and work in a sector and region outside of their home state and current field of interest. This was to fulfill one of the scheme's other main objectives: bringing unity to a nation that had just experienced a violent civil war and in which discrimination and prejudice continued to be an issue. By sending individuals to different states, it was hoped that they would develop a deeper understanding of the religious, cultural, and traditional practices of some of the many other diverse ethnic groups that made up Nigeria, thus forging common ties among the youth community where there had previously been distrust and isolation. The reconciliation and reintegration of Nigeria's different tribes were just as important to the founders of the NYSC as the labor of reconstructing the country's ineffective or damaged infrastructure.

However, there were some other more practical aims as well. Employers of the youth corp members were encouraged to offer permanent jobs at the end of the year of service to help tackle some of the issues with unemployment. Graduates were given important work experience in practical situations which they may not otherwise have been able to find, thus improving their skill level and employability at any company. It was also expected that a year of working and living in a different state would promote the free movement of this highly skilled workforce across the whole country, motivating graduates to seek careers in all areas rather than being concentrated around the major cities or in the more prosperous regions. Being such a large, populous nation, equality and uniformity were hard to achieve.

It was in pursuit of these noble aims that Tony found himself undertaking a long bus journey right across the country. He was sent to Sokoto, in the far northwestern corner of Nigeria, to complete his year of service. This unknown city was hundreds of miles away from both his family in Jos and the town of Ekpoma where he had attended university. Sitting by the window, his small suitcase clasped between his legs, Tony watched the topography and traditional dress of local communities frequently change. It was his first visit to this part of Nigeria, and he eagerly soaked up the variations in landscape and scenery along the way. As was typical for Tony, he found himself instinctively assessing the commercial opportunities and makeup of the towns and cities that he passed through, scrutinizing marketplaces, shopfronts, and farms through his vista inside the bus.

The closer he got to Sokoto, the more he could feel the change in temperature, beads of sweat beginning to form in the small of his back and along his forehead. It has one of the hottest climates in the country—very different from the cooler, temperate one where he grew up in Jos.

As the journey continued, he was also able to observe that the inhabitants were predominantly of Muslim faith, the women often wearing the *hijab* over their hair. It was also clearly one of the more homogenous states, unlike the Plateau State where Jos was located. Whilst the major language was Hausa, which Tony was luckily familiar with from his youth, the customs, culture, and region were very far outside the realm of his previous experiences—exactly in line with the aim of the NYSC program. Although many would have balked at being so far from their family and comfort zone, Tony, typically, saw this challenge as an opportunity. When he finally disembarked from the bus into the bustle of central Sokoto, arriving in this unknown city on his own, he was excited rather than intimidated. He was able to reframe the distance in his mind and concentrate on the benefits that it could offer him.

Although one of the aims of the program was to broaden the practical experience of its participants, Tony secured his first job in the finance sector during this year, working as a teller in one of the banks in the middle of the city. During media interviews, Tony is often quoted praising the role that luck has played in his journey from humble beginnings to a global powerhouse alongside his hard work and single-mindedness. His service is perhaps one such example because he was given the opportunity to work at the Union Bank of Nigeria in Sokoto, even though he could technically have been posted to any role or business type. Many of his fellow graduates were not lucky enough to secure positions in their preferred industries. Tony, meanwhile, was able to gain valuable experience of the daily workings and interactions inside a bank during his experience as a teller. The skill and insight this role provided arguably had a significant impact on his pathway later on.

It was a lively place to work, with a wide range of customers filling the building during opening hours. Tony enjoyed the routine of his work at the counter each day, as well as the diversity of the people he would meet and speak to during the course of his shift. His tasks and responsibilities remained the same, but the customers he interacted with were not, and this gave him an appreciation of the importance of clear communication in business. He also enjoyed observing the unfamiliar culture and social customs around him, soaking up the experience both at work and during the weekends and evenings. He often spent long hours in the bank but would still take the time to walk among the market stalls afterward, considering the relative potential of the wares they sold to make a profit. He was not an entrepreneur yet, but he already knew how to think like one.

In fact, Tony's very first entrepreneurial venture began in Sokoto during his NYSC year. It was during one of his many contemplative walks around the city that he came up with an idea. Sokoto was well-known for tailors who could sew elegant *Babaringa*—a local costume made up of three pieces: a cap, trousers, and a large, free-flowing robe. It was a local flamboyant variation of the *Agbada* that was very popular throughout the whole of Nigeria; Tony had often seen people wearing these outfits in both the Plateau and Bendel states. By conducting research into the prices at the market, he realized that they were sold for a much cheaper price in this part of the country than they were elsewhere. He also knew that he would be able to purchase them for an even more attractive price if he bought from the local traders or tailors in bulk. Thus, Tony's first business venture was formed: His model was to buy the local clothes, along with handmade mats, in Sokoto and then sell them on for a profit to friends in the south of the country whenever he was able to make the long journey back again.

It was a success. The money he earned was a welcome addition to the small stipend provided by the government during his volunteer work as a teller, which only just covered his living expenses in Sokoto. However, the significance of this moment on Tony's journey to success encompassed more than just its ability to provide a supplement for his day-to-day income. He put as much of the modest profit as he could into a bank account. Little by little, the balance grew as the savings accumulated. Watching this process, and keeping track of it, gave Tony his first taste of the excitement of making money. At times, when he felt his motivation waning over the following years, Tony would often think back on the fascination he felt at this first business endeavor and feel energized as a result.

The Copier Salesman

After he had completed his service and obtained his certificate of discharge from the NYSC, Tony returned to the south of the country to try his luck in the banking sector as a salaried employee. He left behind the northwestern corner of Nigeria that he had called home for the last year and moved to Lagos after a brief visit with his family in Jos. On the bus, traveling back across the country once more, Tony studied the changing landscape and towns that passed him by on the other side of his window, recalling his journey in the opposite direction the year before, and contemplating the ways in which his service had helped him in his plan to relocate to the city. Although he knew some graduates and other acquaintances who had tried their luck in Lagos, he didn't have any close friends or family there at the time. In many ways, this move would be just as challenging as the one to Sokoto—in both cases, Tony was basically striking out on his own, a prospector in search of riches. This boldness was characteristic of Tony's confidence and resilience—after all, being daring had already been proven to reap rewards—but it was also indicative of the mindset of many of Nigeria's youth at the time. They were flooding into the big cities, hoping for a change of fortune, for themselves and for their nation as a whole.

The most populous city in Nigeria, and one of the largest in the whole of sub-Saharan Africa, Lagos was the nation's capital in the 1980s, before the decision was taken to replace it with the more geographically central city of Abuja in 1991. Because of its large population and position on the Gulf of Guinea, Lagos has been a hub for trade and development throughout the region's history and has continued to represent progress, business, and opportunity for many Nigerians, even after it lost its status as the capital. It began as a fishing settlement but quickly became an important point of arrival and departure for European slave traders in West Africa because of its coastal location. During the colonial period, Lagos was designated variously as a separate state, part of Nigeria, and part of the colony of West Africa, but it was returned to the control of the Republic of Nigeria conclusively once independence was achieved in 1960. Lagos then became the seat of most of the federal and administrative agencies and, thus, the newly independent nation's power. It became the jewel in

Nigeria's crown—a way to show the world what the country could look like outside of British control—and new buildings and districts were planned accordingly to showcase this and help the city grow. From grand central squares with glistening fountains to bridges and marinas, along with luxury hotels to accommodate visiting foreign dignitaries, the federal government wanted Lagos to shine on an international stage.

Spread across a number of islands, sandbars, and lagoons, the city has an interesting topography that makes it unique. Rising along the edge of the turquoise waters are a mixture of imposing colonial structures and modern erections. Because Lagos was so integral to Nigeria's identity as an independent nation, it quickly became an economic powerhouse. Manufacturers ranging from textiles to beverages to cars have long been drawn to the area because of the city's port at Apapa Quay and the availability of cheap labor. It thus became Nigeria's center for commerce and industry as a result. Similarly, workers began to pour into the city when it was officially named as the capital in the 1960s, hoping to leave behind the poverty and lack of opportunities that were experienced in many of the rural areas of the country, establishing the link between Lagos and progress which still exists today. The University of Lagos was one of the oldest institutions in the country, established in 1962, and had a strong academic reputation. It was also a huge draw for the young and ambitious, ensuring that the mass migration to the city continued over the long term and increasingly included a skilled workforce and entrepreneurs as well. It is now the second fastest-growing city in Africa and the seventh fastest in the world. It boasts the highest skyline in the country, with both business growth and overcrowding driving an increase in the number of multistory buildings along the coastline, jostling for position among the remnants of the city's 2,000-year history.

In the 1980s, when Tony moved there to seek his fortune, it was at the heart of the oil-fuelled prosperity which was happening at the time, as well as the rise in the number and profitability of the banks. As a result, there was money around and a boom in the culture and nightlife scenes. New venues opened to accommodate this growth, and the city of Lagos became a hub for music, films, and partying. The new technology which had begun to evolve in the music and film industries worldwide during the 1970s, coupled with an increase in the number of

American movies and artists which flooded the city in the following decade, led to an atmosphere of innovation and creativity. Young Nigerians embraced the rising funk music scene, which was exciting and aspirational.

It was a time when many residents of Lagos were making money, spending money, and going out. They enjoyed dressing to impress, looking good, and embracing the success of the new urban scene. If you were to walk along Broad Street, on Lagos Island, in the early 1980s, you would see this in evidence all around you. Everything from the mixture of traditional dress with Western fashion and the heavily-laden bicycles alongside sleek new cars to the woven baskets of produce being sold on the steps of offices and the glass-fronted banks built between resplendent stone churches and old-fashioned houses encapsulated the image of a new Nigeria. At all times of day and night, Broad Street was crowded and colorful—an exciting place for the young Tony Elumelu, who would soak in the feel of change and progress after he moved to the city.

Such rapid growth, however, also had a dark underbelly: Slums grew just as quickly as skyscrapers with the arrival of so many impoverished workers without the infrastructure to support them. Many of those who migrated to Lagos did so without savings, housing, or a job offer; they were simply attracted to the draw of the big city, like bees seeking nectar, desperate to escape the cycle of hardship that existed in rural areas. Although they could often find work in the factories, it was informal, with no contracts or protection offered, and so, the escape from poverty that they dreamed of was not always forthcoming. Thousands simply traded a life in poverty in the countryside for a life in poverty in the city. Similarly, although the government plowed money and resources into buildings and projects which furthered the image of Lagos that they wished to perpetuate, they did not put enough into schools, hospitals, housing, or transport, and so, the city's levels of inequality rocketed. There was also an increasing problem with pollution from the growth in traffic and the number of factories—another cost of Lagos's development.

With his sights still centered on the fashionable life of the banker adorned with suspenders and brogues, Tony set himself apart from many of the other migrants who arrived in Lagos. Firstly, he had a clear goal and a plan. More importantly, he had a small but significant sum in his savings account from his first business venture selling the suits and baskets from Sokoto. This allowed him to secure a small apartment on the outskirts of the commercial district and establish a foothold in the city despite the competitive housing market, setting him up in his first year. With this serving as a base and security, Tony was able to embrace the atmosphere of possibility and opportunity that the city's rapid growth created, instead of falling victim to some of its disadvantages. But even though he had a good undergraduate degree, a year of volunteering experience as a teller, and his apartment, he was still just one of thousands of graduates who had opted to make the city their home. He was smart, determined, hardworking, and ambitious, but so were many of the other new arrivals, and finance was rapidly becoming the most popular career avenue for educated young Nigerians because of the increase in the number of banks lining the glamorous Broad Street.

After a few months of disappointment and no success in his hunt for suitable employment, Tony decided to regroup and improve his chances for the future. Thanks to his modest savings, he was not put off from his eventual goal nor discouraged enough to leave Lagos or forced to apply for a job doing menial labor like many other thwarted graduates. Instead, he decided to return to academia. His strong belief in the power of education, instilled in him by his parents, encouraged him to apply for a Master's degree program in Economics at the University of Lagos. Before his year of national service, he had contemplated the option of continuing on at university, so this move didn't feel out of sync with his goals. Tony hoped that this additional year of study would help him to both stand out in the crowded labor market during job applications and improve his understanding of the contemporary intricacies of the country's commercial and financial situation; the more that Nigeria was changing before his eyes, the more Tony could see the benefits of having the most up-to-date academic and theoretical knowledge behind the work that he hoped to undertake.

As one of the first tertiary educational institutions to be established in Nigeria, the University of Lagos played an important role in the growth of many of the nation's commercial and industrial sectors, quickly gaining a reputation for quality teaching and research-led programs.

Tony knew that it was an achievement in and of itself to be accepted onto a postgraduate course there, particularly in a subject as sought-after as economics. He re-entered the world of academia in search of the knowledge that would lead him to a successful career in banking and enjoyed both high-quality education and advice from excellent tutors over the following year. At the same time, his age and real-life experience in the NYSC meant that he approached the year with a slightly different perspective to his undergraduate degree: Tony was able to use his analytical mind to hone in on the expertise and information that he recognized as most important in practice outside of his studies. Thanks to his entrepreneurial spirit and small apartment, he was also able to live a lifestyle that was more akin to a worker than a student, enjoying the range of music, culture, and nightlife that living in Nigeria's most populous city had to offer.

But although he furthered his knowledge substantially during his Master's education, it did not immediately yield the result he was hoping for in terms of employment in the banking sector. Despite his year of experience as a teller in Sokoto and two degrees, he was unable to secure work in a bank in Lagos after graduation, even when applying to the more lowly positions—the market was just too full.

No stranger to hard work, having exerted himself through long shifts in his mother's restaurant during his youth and busy hours at the counter in Sokoto, Tony decided to seek salaried employment in as many companies as he could and gain some more experience in the business world to better support his applications for finance positions. His resilience and persistence came to fruition at last, and he secured a job as a copier salesman. It was still a relatively lowly—and low paying—job, but Tony was grateful for the chance to learn more about commerce in Lagos in any capacity after so many disappointments since his move to the city. Just as he did when he was helping his mother or reading newspapers and magazines, he spent much of his indefatigable energy considering the wider context of the sales and business of industry as a whole, in addition to his daily tasks. He would often spend his evenings in his little apartment, watching the bustle of Lagos outside, listening to the constant thrum of the traffic on the streets and the sharp beep of the horns, analyzing profit and loss margins in his notebook, sometimes even dreaming up ways to improve the copier company's overall viability and what strategies he would pursue if he was in the role of its CEO. This all helped him to stay focused on his path for the future, rather than allowing himself to become satisfied with the modest income and responsibilities in the role that he had secured, and thus, he continued to dream and dare to achieve much more. Eating cheap meals from the nearby market and surrounded by the mismatched furniture that came in situ with the apartment, Tony was confident that this was only the beginning of his career. He could achieve more; he could work at one of the new banks on Broad Street, adding his own footsteps to the ebb and flow of traffic along its sidewalks, and live in one of the luxurious new buildings with views over the sparkling lagoon, rather his current view of the dingy streets below.

This job as a copier salesman was also an excellent opportunity for him to develop his communication skills as he conversed with a diverse range of customers and traveled to different areas of the city. Like all his ventures, Tony's brief sales career was a success: He had a natural ability to find a connection with a potential customer, and his honesty, integrity, and persistence endeared him to his clients. The more he journeyed across Lagos and made his way in and out of office buildings to meet with them, the more he became comfortable in different businesses and meetings, feeling more and more at ease in this world. Without a doubt, he could have prevailed in this industry and moved up the ranks if he had so desired. However, almost a year after his Master's degree, he found an opportunity at one of the new-generation banks and never looked back.

A Lucky Chance

It was Tony's routine to scour newspapers and magazines for job advertisements and postings each morning over a coffee and a simple breakfast meal of bread, eggs, or rice. Although he had his regular income from working as a salesman, he never lost sight of his ambition to work in finance. Applications continued to be an incredibly competitive process—especially as an increase in the number of universities and places was thus producing more and more skilled graduates—but Tony did not let this diminish his hope. Where some might have been content working in sales, Tony continued to seek and apply for suitable positions in banks whenever he saw them, rising early to complete this task each day before he set off around the city for his work. He would head out early to the kiosks, enjoying the relative peace and quiet in the morning light—as much as such a bustling city is ever peaceful or quiet—and collect the day's papers to read in his apartment. As he was such a regular and good customer, Tony endeared himself to the newspaper sellers, just as he did to his clients in the copier industry, and they would often keep a stack of papers aside for him.

During one such morning perusal of the Lagos papers, on an ordinary day about a year after graduating from the University of Lagos, Tony came across a one-page advertisement for an entry-level financial analyst at Allstates Trust Bank. The sight of its logo gave Tony an immediate frisson of excitement: It was one of the new generation of banks that had been set up in the financial boom of the 1980s, just the sort of institution that he could envisage giving a candidate like him a chance. But the advert clearly stated the requirements for the position, which included a minimum of a 2.1 qualification (upper second class honors) for applicants' undergraduate degrees. Tony felt his heart sink as quickly as his hopes had risen; he had graduated with a 2.2 (lower second class honors) degree from Bendel State University in Economics. On paper, he didn't meet the criteria.

He spent the rest of the day, as he went about his usual tasks and routine, thinking about the job advertisement. For some unknown reason, it felt like a moment of destiny for Tony. He felt drawn to this particular job, even though he didn't hold the level of qualification they were looking for, and even though he had applied for numerous other entry-level positions in the previous two years since arriving in Lagos. Perhaps, it was the fact that this particular bank encapsulated everything that attracted Tony to Nigeria's banking sector. Perhaps, it was just that Tony felt that his time, surely, after so much hard work and the stalwart way he had applied for various jobs and written various letters of application, had finally come.

Allstates Trust Bank was new: It was founded in 1988 by a group of investors led by Ebitimi E. Banigo, who set up the bank's headquarters on Victoria Island in Lagos. This affluent area was one of the busiest and fastest growing areas of the city where many Nigerian and international companies were locating their most prominent offices. With such prosperity abounding, it also became a center for finance and one of the most expensive places to buy or rent property. It was clear that the bank's trustees had high ambitions for their new venture. With an MBA from Harvard and experience managing another high-profile bank, Banigo was well-placed to deliver on these expectations and quickly grow a reputable, well-managed institution. For Tony, it was too good an opportunity to pass up.

That evening, Tony made his decision: Even though he didn't technically have the requisite qualifications, he was going to make an application and write a cover letter that explained why he was nonetheless right for the position. Sitting hunched over his pen and paper at the wooden table in his tiny kitchen area, Tony wrote several drafts of the letter before he was finally satisfied with the result. He signed it with a flourish, then stood up and stretched his arms to the ceiling in order to release the tension that had come from several hours of sitting in one place. He placed the finished letter and other documentation in an envelope, addressed it to the CEO of the bank, and then left it propped on the counter for delivery the following day.

In the morning, rather than collecting the newspapers as usual, Tony set out for work earlier than routine would dictate, taking the letter with him. He did not want to trust the postal service with such important cargo, so he made the journey across the lagoon to Victoria Island himself. When the headquarters opened, he delivered it in person. Afterward, heart still racing, he had a strong feeling that he was hovering right on the cusp of change. He was right: It was at this point in his journey that fortune smiled on Tony.

In the years since, Tony has spoken and written extensively about the importance of hard work, commitment, and drive in achieving success; but he is also candid about the role that luck has played in his journey. It is another quality that marks Tony out from his peers as so exceptional. In most cases, the role that luck plays within business is very often ignored, or derided, as it is usually seen as belonging in opposition to hard work. If luck is discussed, many people think, it seems to undermine or dismiss the diligence which has happened alongside it. To call someone "lucky," in the business world is to diminish their sense of personal achievement. Yet, Tony's honesty and integrity allow him to talk about luck as much as perseverance. The application to Allstates Trust Bank—the job which started him on the path to real success—was one such example of how luck was also important for him. "It is simply not true," Tony states, "that you make your own luck in the world" (Elumelu, 2019).

Tony's stroke of luck here was that his application was personally received by the bank's chairman and that Ebitimi was a precise and thorough worker. He was the sort of man who painstakingly read each cover letter and application himself. A few days after Tony made his delivery, the chairman settled down at his desk to review the thick stack of applications that had been collated by his assistant. It was a time-consuming process to read and review each one so thoroughly, but Ebitimi was not in a hurry; he was more interested in finding the right candidate to join the community of employees at his bank than in a speedy recruitment process.

Thanks to the prominent advertisement that they had put out, they received hundreds of letters and resumes from interested graduates. As the chairman read through them, one by one, he was struck by the fact that, although they were almost universally of high quality, they were also factual, staid, and rather unadventurous. Too many of the candidates seemed to be going through the motions and applying for the job with the same stock words or phrases that they had used in other applications. Ebitimi was aware that the job market was very tough for young people in such an overcrowded city and appreciated that many of them would be applying unsuccessfully for jobs each week, leading them to feel disheartened. But, on paper at least, they lacked the spark of passion that he was looking to add to his bank. He envisaged this role as a long-term one. Even though this was for an entry-level position initially, he was ideally seeking a candidate whom he could mentor as the bank grew.

Towards the end of the pile, trying not to feel frustrated that he had only selected a few people to interview so far, Ebitimi came across Tony's application. He was about to dismiss it quite quickly, having at last grown weary of the process and seeing that the candidate did not have the relevant undergraduate degree, when he spotted the envelope in which it had arrived, which had been paper-clipped behind the letter and resume. There was no postage mark, and he was impressed that Tony had made the effort to deliver it himself. This gave Ebitimi pause, and he decided to read the letter in full (Okwumbu-Imafidon, 2022):

> "I know I may not have met the qualifying criteria for the advertised roles, but I am intelligent, driven, ambitious, and I will make the bank proud. My 2.2 degree does not demonstrate the full extent of my intelligence and ability, and I know I can do so much more."

It was exactly the sort of passion, confidence, and ambition that he had been looking for. Ebitimi read it again, then carefully placed the letter and resume at the top of the much smaller pile of shortlisted candidates. Tony's gamble paid off: The chairman had decided to give this young, intelligent man a chance, even though he didn't meet the criteria.

In some ways, of course, this is evidence of Tony making his own luck. The very fact that he submitted the application demonstrated that he was relying on his skill, ability, and perseverance to help him gain opportunities. But the fact that his application was reviewed by a man who shared his vision and who was willing to give someone unknown a chance to further present his suitability at an interview, was equally as important—and lucky.

It was another week before Tony received the good news. He had had the application to AllStates Trust Bank in the back of his mind ever since completing it, still struck by the notion that this role was meant for him. When he let himself into his apartment that evening to find a letter waiting, his pulse began to thrum. The bank's logo was stamped in the top corner, and Tony felt that same sense of awareness and excitement that he had felt when first reading the advertisement. When he saw that he had received an invitation to join the shortlisted candidates, he was delighted and let out a shout of joy that surely disturbed his neighbors in the building.

Once the initial elation had died down, Tony became determined to ensure that this opportunity would yield the desired outcome. He changed his routine, staying up late and spending long hours preparing for the interview at AllStates Trust Bank, rather than rising early to collect the newspapers. He carefully planned his outfit and appearance during the wait for the next stage of the recruitment process. He considered how to radiate confidence and ambition from the first meeting, settling on his smartest suit and brogues, which he polished to a high shine. At the last minute, he decided he looked too formal and conservative, and he added a subtle splash of color with red socks.

Nerves and anticipation mounting, he made his way to Victoria Island once again, having taken leave from his sales job for the day. What followed was long, arduous, and rigorous: The shortlisted applicants were put through their paces with a long series of interviews and tests to determine their capability and potential. They were grilled and appraised in every way possible, and Tony was up against tough competition.

Eventually, however, the tests were finished, and Tony was the recipient of good news: He had been given the job as an entry-level financial analyst at the bank. His career as a salaried employee working in the finance industry had finally begun, and he celebrated with gusto.

He often—especially during the first few whirlwind months of working at AllStates Trust Bank—thought back on what had helped him achieve that first crucial step up on his career ladder. He remained eternally grateful to the chairman who had taken a chance on him, and they developed a close relationship once he was appointed. He would also reflect, at many different moments in later life, on the luck that had helped him to those positions, wondering how different his life may have turned out if the chairman had not personally read his application; if he'd decided not to apply after all; if the application had been rejected outright for failing to meet the desired qualification; if he had never been awarded the job. How, he would think, might his life have been different as a result?

Tony's single-minded determination and commitment suggest that he would doubtless have received an opportunity in banking eventually. But it was this particular bank, hiring an ambitious young Tony Elumelu, at that particular moment, not long after being founded, which arguably contributed most to the direction and momentum of his path to success. It was an important step for him, but also one that had a significant impact on his business philosophy and values. He has, since that lucky chance that spurred on his own story, believed in the power of luck and has been committed to spreading its power to others wherever and whenever he can.

Chapter 3:

Banking Career

The Youngest Branch Manager

The beginning of Tony's banking career, and the continuation of Tony's story, really takes off at AllStates Trust Bank. Having been given such an important opportunity personally by the founder of this new generation bank, Tony was determined both to ensure the chance was not wasted and that the chairman's confidence in him was not unfounded. He threw himself into his role as an entry-level analyst with the passion he had demonstrated in his cover letter, embracing the image, lifestyle, and mindset of banking with every fiber of his being. It was, after all, the fulfillment of a dream that he had had since the start of the decade.

It was a very different role to his experience as a teller in Sokoto, which had been the sum of his experience working in a bank day to day. He was now working behind the scenes rather than in a front-of-house position dealing with customers. Although this position was entry-level, he was given the opportunity to assist and work alongside senior financial analysts in all aspects of their job, such as evaluating company budgets and assets. He was also tasked with creating and maintaining records, generating reports, and working on a range of projects. It was an exciting window into the world of finance for Tony and everything that he had hoped it would be when he first chose to study economics for his undergraduate degree and dreamed of the lifestyle of the banker, living the high life in Lagos.

Over the course of the following year, Tony worked hard as an analyst to demonstrate the qualities that he outlined in his application letter: intelligence, drive, ambition, and dedication. He wanted to make the bank, and the chairman who had believed in him in particular, proud of his achievements.

Just as Tony was an outstanding student during his school and university days and a strong copy salesman the year before, he excelled in his first role in banking. He was unfailingly energetic and one of the first employees to volunteer to tackle or take on challenging tasks. He gave priority to getting things done and meeting deadlines. Within a short space of time, and despite his relatively junior level within the structure of the bank's hierarchy, he became known as both a safe pair of hands and someone who delivered results. He was careful not to over-promise on his ability or experience, but his innate intelligence and problem-solving skills meant that he was able to see innovative and creative solutions where other analysts could not. As his reputation grew, Ebitimi Banigo—who had, of course, handpicked him for the interview—began to take more and more notice of the success and energy that Tony brought to his role. Needless to say, Ebitimi was not disappointed by his choice of candidate and the chance they had taken on offering Tony an interview without the requisite 2.1 degree. It was a clear example for the chairman that numbers and paperwork cannot tell you the full story of an individual's potential and ability—exactly the reason why he had so dedicatedly and painstakingly reviewed each of the applications that were made for the position in his bank.

After 12 months of impressing both the founder and his boss, Toyin Akin-Johnson, Tony received another exciting opportunity at AllStates Trust Bank. He was called into a meeting with the two managers to find out that, despite the incredibly short time that he had been working at the bank and his relative inexperience after just a year of practical work in this field, they wanted to promote him further. They outlined their belief in Tony and his future career, and they took another chance on this exceptional young man from Jos who had already so impressed them: They appointed Tony as branch manager. AllStates Trust Bank was still new at the time—having only just been set up in 1988—and this bold move by Tony's managers was indicative of the success of the financial industry as a whole in the context of an unpredictable national economy. Just as he did when he set up a new bank in the first place, Ebitimi Banigo took a gamble and made an investment. The investment, this time, was in Tony: He was betting that Tony Elumelu would reap success and profit for his bank in the future. Tony was the exact type of candidate that Ebitimi had been hoping to recruit for the entry-level position: one that would offer them rewards in the long term through his commitment to the institution that helped him get a foot on the ladder in the first place, and one who was eager to be mentored and molded into their ideal type of employee.

The rise to the position of bank manager was a significant one for Tony, not least in the way in which it propelled him several rungs further up the career ladder. The promotion allowed him to leap over a number of intermediate positions—as well as many employees with more experience in banking than he had—and go straight into a leadership role. Ebitimi and Akin-Johnson knew that Tony was less experienced than some, but they recognized that he had the raw qualities of an inspirational leader, even if he was not yet fully formed in this way. With the amount of effort and energy that he put into his work, Tony was certainly well-deserving of a promotion, but he was also lucky, just as he was to be offered the interview at the bank in the first place, and he owed his bosses a debt of gratitude for noticing him and giving him such a chance. At 27, therefore, Tony became the youngest ever branch manager at the time. It was the start of a number of historic milestones that Tony achieved.

The bank manager role was very different from that of an analyst, and it gave Tony the opportunity to hone a different skill set which ultimately opened the door to other top leadership positions. In this position, Tony oversaw every aspect of the office's operations, including hiring or firing employees, overseeing loans and credit notes, managing business and customer relations, and ensuring that the branch's goals and objectives were met. He was responsible for managing all parts of the day-to-day functioning and revenue of his branch, as well as a large number of employees—quite a step up from assisting senior analysts on some of the elements of reporting and strategy behind the scenes at the bank. It was a huge leap of faith on the part of his bosses because, in essence, Tony was responsible for the success or failure of that entire branch of the bank. Due to this level of responsibility, branch managers usually have a wealth of experience in operation management or a proven track record as a manager in order to be appointed. Tony was, in essence, the CEO of his own branch. Yet, he did not allow himself to be daunted by the task ahead of him. His ability to multitask, prioritize effectively, analyze potential problems, and focus on details made him a natural in the role. The fact that he was charming and personable also helped because the tellers and other employees liked being managed by him and were willing to work collectively towards the success of the branch.

As the youngest branch manager in the company, Tony was also somewhat reknowned among the employees, and the customers, of the bank. He enjoyed the challenge—and the notoriety—that the role afforded him. In many ways, however, although it was the first significant role in his banking career, it was only a stepping stone to greater success. The experience it offered, nevertheless, was invaluable, and the status he achieved as the youngest employee to hold the post similarly helped to open doors to further leadership roles in the future.

It also left its mark on his philosophical approach to the world and his philanthropic work: Tony has been determined to offer young Africans his support and expertise and to help open the door for them into the world of business in this way, just as he himself was supported by the two men who took a chance on him in his first role in finance. In this way, Banigo's mentorship and support of young talents like Tony have had a lasting impact on Nigeria's banking sector; his influence on the industry and individuals, including Tony himself, cannot be underestimated as a result. Even though he is retired from actively running a bank, Ebitimi Banigo continues to inspire Nigerian bankers as a forward-thinking banker who was ahead of the times.

The Cowboys of Banking

During his tenure as branch manager for AllStates Trust Bank, Tony saw firsthand just how much effort it took to succeed in the banking world, and he was inspired by the dedication he saw in his bosses. The tasks and obstacles that he encountered in his work, both in terms of the daily running and functioning of the branch and the intricacies of the financial sector as a whole given Nigeria's unpredictable economy, taught him valuable lessons and skills which he took with him into the future.

Furthermore, as he grew in confidence and reputation, he made a point of connecting with each of his bosses so that they became his mentors. He learned from their experiences and insights as well as his own. He also quickly came to understand that success in business could depend on the relationships and networks that you could build. He saw, through his own personal opportunities and the interactions between coworkers, that success often depended on who you knew and how you could leverage those relationships to achieve your goals. Tony could see the power of relationships in the banking world, and this was one of the lessons that had the greatest impact on his journey. This appreciation of the importance of business relationships led Tony to the next stage of his career.

While he was working at AllStates Trust Bank, he began to build strong connections with his peers and soon formed friendships with a group of young, ambitious, and determined bankers just like himself. It started out casually enough, seeking each other out over coffee or lunch breaks, where they would converse about the challenges and successes they had faced during their working days. The group included Jim Ovia, Aigboje Aig-Imoukhuede, Herbert Wigwe, and Fola Adeola—all relatively unknown figures in Nigerian banking who would go on to found a number of other leading financial institutions, including Zenith Bank, Access Bank, and Guaranty Trust Bank, playing crucial roles in the sector. But even at the time, they were respected for taking risks, being innovative, and helping to transform the sector into a more dynamic and competitive landscape.

And their plans grew, one evening, into something much more daring. Over a beer or two, the group of young bankers discussed their frustrations at some of the management decisions that had been made at the banks where they worked in recent months. They shared strategies that they would have chosen to follow instead and why they believed these would have been more successful than what their bosses had chosen to do. They talked, in vague terms, about a bright day in the future in which they might achieve positions much higher up the food chain and, thus, have a say in these kinds of big-ticket moments, rather than having to ultimately follow the direction that their superiors wanted their branches or departments to take. The friends clinked glasses—a celebration of their ambition and ideas but also an unspoken pact that they would achieve such success together.

Tony was, in many ways, the leader of the little group of friends that had formed through networking events and meetings in the financial sector. When he walked home that night from the bar in the ever-present heat, his eyes were drawn upward to some of the new construction happening on the mainland in the distance. For now, in the dark, the cranes and cement mixers were silent, but he could make out the silhouettes of their hulking shapes. He thought he could see the glow of lights from the exclusive Lagos Country Club beside the building works, or perhaps, it was a reflected sparkle from the windows of the tall, slim international hotels that ringed them. It must be Ikeja that he was looking at—the most expensive, sought-after residential area in the city.

Despite the sweltering weather, he felt drawn towards Ikeja. He walked and walked, all the time thinking about the conversation that had been had that evening. He felt the same buzz of anticipation that he had felt when he saw the newspaper advertisement for the job at AllStates Trust Bank, as if this moment was a significant turning point in his life—as if this was the right moment, and he was the right man, to make this happen.

Eventually, he reached the broad avenues of Ikeja. Here, the night did not feel as humid or oppressively hot. The sidewalks and roads did not seem to absorb and reflect the heat in the same way that the tarmac and concrete in the center of the city always did. Perhaps, it was the abundance of foliage and trees in this neighborhood, the width of the streets, or the gardens and spaces between the residences. Maybe, it was simply the result of only sporadic traffic—a far cry from the constant movement outside his own apartment. He stopped to admire a newly built detached house, its exterior shining bright white. He could almost imagine how cool, quiet, and comfortable it would be inside.

At last, Tony turned back for home, only then realizing just how far he had come, lost in his reverie. He began looking for a taxi with its light on to take him back to his current apartment. It was much more spacious than his first accommodations in Lagos, but it could not compare to the sprawling properties and tree-lined streets of Ikeja.

The next morning, Tony woke early, despite his lack of sleep. He felt energized and determined. He put a call through to his friends to ask them to meet in the same bar that evening. When he replaced the receiver into its cradle, he thought again of the new white house in Ikeja. As the manager of his branch, he was, in essence, playing the role of CEO—albeit on a small scale. It was not such a stretch to envision himself in the highest role in a bank instead.

When he shared his plan with his group of his friends, however, there was some nervous laughter in response. They weren't well-known in banking in Nigeria, outside of their small circle of influence and their mentors. How could they possibly take over a bank on their own? But they had one important thing in common: They were determined to make history. And they knew that they could trust Tony's vision and instincts. As he began to share his 10-year plan for building a successful bank and his strategy of how to acquire one, they leaned forward eagerly, heads nodding. Now, they dared to believe it was possible— they dared to dream that they could do it. It took careful planning, preparation, and patience, but in 1997, they made an audacious move that propelled them all into the limelight.

Despite Tony's success at AllStates Trust Bank and the continued rise in the number of financial institutions in Lagos, Nigeria, as a whole, was characterized by instability and insecurity during the 1990s. The economy continued to be unpredictable, partly because of the volatility of the political situation. The country vacillated between support for the democratic process and reliance on the army, which it saw as the only way to unite the many diverse peoples and factions in Nigeria, despite its record of harsh, corrupt rule since independence in 1960. The result was a period of regular protests, bursts of violence, and several major coups d'etat. Control moved back and forth between elected officials and military leaders, which made the economy even more volatile. Perhaps unsurprisingly, many of the new generation of banks struggled within this context, especially as many lacked the experienced managers and expert investment strategies needed to prosper under such challenging and constantly changing circumstances.

Having carefully studied the ebbs and flows within the sector and the way that it reacted to external and economic changes, Tony and his friends in the industry predicted that many of the new banks established since the late 1980s—which had nearly all been set up without proper consideration or leadership as part of the initial boom in demand and profitability for this service—would be unable to survive beyond the end of the decade. This is where Tony's patience and analytical skills came into their own. In order to carry out the takeover that they had planned together, the group had to wait for, and find, just the right institution for it all to come to fruition. They scrutinized the financial news and reports religiously, ready to pounce when the right opportunity presented itself to them.

By the end of the 1990s, their prediction about the new generation of banks was proven correct, and a number of them stood on the brink of collapse. Now, it was a question of finding one with a suitable balance of debt, investment, and potential. It was one such institution—Crystal Bank—which Tony and his peers set their sights on.

It took much of the financial sector by surprise when this group of young, hungry outsiders bid to acquire the distressed bank. Some considered them bold; others considered them foolish. It earned them the nickname "the cowboys of banking." But whilst their critics may have wished to label them dishonest, careless, irresponsible, or lacking in skill through this choice of name, Tony and his fellow investors embraced the positive qualities which it conferred on them. After all, they were not following the established rules that most people obeyed in the industry. But their move was not reckless, although it was risky and bold, and instead, they came to embody the brave, tough characteristics of the cowboy. Their proposal was simple enough: They wanted to take over the running of a bank that was facing liquidation, and they had a clear, well-thought-out strategy ready to rescue it.

Some of the stakeholders were interested to hear their plans, even though they were still relatively inexperienced and unknown. After all, without this bold "cowboy" move, they were potentially facing huge losses, and here was a group of young men who were proposing that they would, in fact, get their money back—even if it would be over a period of time. Not all of the bank's investors wanted to be part of Tony's restructuring of their assets and debts, deeming it too unpredictable and new at a time when instability in the country was already rife. They chose to withdraw as much of their principal investment as they could instead. But enough of the investors were prepared to listen and see what this new group of financiers could accomplish when given the chance, and so, a formal application to the Central Bank of Nigeria was made by Tony and his friends to take control of Crystal Bank.

They had been equipped for taking this gamble by the encouragement and exposure they had received from superiors and mentors. Tony, in particular, felt prepared for this scale of a challenge as a result of the learning opportunities he had received at AllStates but also the benevolence of his superiors. It fueled his self-belief, and the trust they put in him drove him to take a chance on the struggling Crystal Bank. Without this sense of preparedness and encouragement behind him, he may not have felt such confidence in taking this next step.

The cowboys' move was not without complications, however. The initial application to the Central Bank of Nigeria was turned down as too bold and spurious. This put the friends firmly in their place: They were too inexperienced, too outlandish in their proposals, and too amateur to run a bank as large and debt-ridden as Crystal Bank, especially without the support or backing of someone with a reputation that was already established in the financial sector. Despite the fact that there were no other offers in place, the Central Bank deemed them too much of a risk.

Disheartened, the friends met in their regular haunt—the same bar in which this plan had initially been conceived of and hashed out, time and again—to regroup. Some wanted to withdraw the offer until they could find a well-known CEO or manager from an existing bank to join their ranks. But Tony showed resilience and perseverance by restrategizing and reforming their ideas as a result of the feedback he received and then insisting on a meeting with the Finance Minister and the Central Bank of Nigeria to discuss their three-tier strategy in more detail. Far from diminishing the ambition that they had shown in the initial proposal, Tony made sure the updated three-tier strategy was even bolder.

The meeting was agreed upon, and just as he had impressed Ebitimi E. Banigo with his letter and then his interview skills, Tony's personable skills and confidence won them over. Standing in front of these powerful men, Tony, in his neatly tailored suit and trademark flash of color—red socks and a matching red tie—was the epitome of the ambition that Nigeria hoped to inspire in its youth after so much conflict and instability. He calmly and coolly stated that he knew exactly what he had to do—and what he could achieve, if given the chance—to turn around the fortunes of Crystal Bank. He outlined how he would do this: Firstly, they would make the bank profitable, then become one of the nation's top 10 banks, and finally become one of the top 3. He anticipated a time range of 10 years for this to be complete. To declare this in the presence of such prominent figures was certainly a risk, but taking this risk is also what set him on his unique path to success. It seemed, at the time, an audacious commitment to make when Crystal Bank was ready to be liquidated and none of the new generation of banks had made it close to entering the ranks of the top 10 financial institutions in Nigeria.

However, just as when his application impressed the founder of AllStates Trust Bank, it was partly Tony's intelligence, skill, and determination which won the "cowboys" ownership of the bank. In the end, both the Finance Minister and the Central Bank of Nigeria backed Tony himself as an investment, as much as the offer that had been made for Crystal Bank. It came down to the fact that, when he spoke, they believed in him—they believed that he could make it happen.

The Youngest CEO

From the youngest branch manager to a "cowboy" of the banking world, Tony was secretly delighted by his notoriety among his coworkers and peers. The move to acquire Crystal Bank gave him a new position of prominence and power that changed the scale and direction of his ambition. They had not forgotten the clink of glasses that began this process and solidified them as a group working toward a common goal; but when they took over the bank, a unanimous decision was made that Tony, who had been the driving force and instigator of the whole process, was appointed as the CEO. He once again made history—this time, as the youngest banking CEO in Nigeria, at the age of just 34.

In most situations and countries, it would be unheard of for a man of this age, with less than a decade of experience within the sector, to be appointed as the head of a bank—especially one that was struggling to survive. Similarly, it would be unheard of for a group of young, unknown people to lead its recovery entirely themselves. But this was where operating in the context of Nigeria, in particular—and Africa, as a whole—opened doors for Tony and his friends. They were able to take advantage of the thirst for change which existed at the end of the 1990s and, thus, undertake a feat that would likely have been impossible in Western nations. As a result of this sudden fame in the business world, the media in Nigeria began to come calling for Tony. He found himself the subject of interviews and requests for quotes from financial journalists in Lagos and beyond. Many were eager to know of his plans for the bank; others were eager to understand how he had made such a meteoric rise to success himself.

As soon as they were granted ownership of the bank, such notoriety was quickly forgotten in the midst of the day-to-day running of their new venture. Tony and his fellow investors dedicated themselves to the difficult task of turning it around, pouring all their energy, drive, and vision into achieving its success. Although Crystal Bank had only been incorporated in 1990, a series of poor management decisions had left it in a dire situation. By 1997, it had low profitability, a low market share in a crowded market, and a lack of direction. In many ways, it might have been easier to start a bank completely from scratch, but this would have involved myriad other challenges in itself. But that was one of the reasons why Crystal Bank was so perfectly situated for their bold, innovative takeover and why they were given the chance by officials to turn it around.

In the role of CEO, however, Tony decided, with his usual breadth of vision and understanding of the market, to take the approach of forming a new company from the remnants of Crystal Bank. Although he took on the few remaining assets of value, such as the existing premises and staff, he otherwise set about rebranding it and rebuilding it from the ground up as if it were a brand-new establishment. Tony knew well, through his own personal experiences as well as in business, the impact that reputation could have on success, and so, their first move was to rename the bank. The investors decided on Standard Trust Bank—a clear, simple, efficient choice, which they hoped would come to be embodied by the services they offered once they had moved the bank into profitability.

It was a journey beset by challenges and setbacks. The Nigerian economy continued to be unstable and unpredictable. Some of the original investors lost patience with the strategy. There were long hours worked by everyone, but especially by Tony. In his office at the headquarters, he would pore over charts and reports for hours, using his keen mind to find the most advantageous niches and trends in which to move his investment. He still read the newspapers each morning with his breakfast, but now he turned straight to the financial pages, not the job advertisements. It was a matter of pride for Tony to keep up with all the twists and turns of commerce and banking in both the country and the continent. It also helped to give him the seeds of ideas about how to grow the bank into the powerhouse he knew it could be. During a period when many businesses and institutions were relying on established methods and areas of investment or trade, Tony was always looking for new, creative ways to mark Standard Trust Bank out from the crowd.

His dedication paid off: By 2004, within just seven short years, Standard Trust Bank had become a household name in Nigeria and one of the fastest-growing, most dynamic banks in the country. Tony had achieved the first two tiers of his strategic goals—and well within the predicted time scale of 10 years.

Tony was crucial to this prosperity. As the CEO, he had the biggest impact on the bank's pathway and strategic vision, and he implemented a series of bold and innovative measures to revitalize the bank. He was responsible for overseeing all operations, particularly the corporate finance and investment banking deals. He successfully built relationships with key stakeholders, brokered brilliant deals, and identified creative opportunities for growth and innovation, including a focus on new technology. The notorious "cowboy" had become a major player in the world of finance. Even their critics were silenced by such success.

But much of the bank's growth can be credited to Tony's vision for equality of opportunity across Nigeria, rather than corporate deals. Whilst many of his competitors continued to focus their efforts and investments on growing in metropolitan areas—and particularly in Lagos, where growth had traditionally been highest thanks to economic migration into the cities—Tony had a different idea. He was determined to expand access to financial services across the whole country in order to increase the opportunities that people in all areas of Nigeria had to achieve their own success. When they first acquired the bank, there was only one isolated branch established in Lagos. But Tony's strategy was to leave the city and this competitive and oversaturated space behind, opening branches across the country instead.

It was a huge success. Almost as soon as branches began opening in different towns and states, demand for their services soared. Too many citizens did not have easy access to bank accounts, electronic payments, and instant transfers before Standard Trust Bank helped to provide them. Rather than having to travel huge distances to complete these everyday tasks, Tony's new banks offered thousands of people the chance to do it quickly and simply near their homes. This was more efficient and cost-effective for many and had a significant impact on many inhabitants of rural areas.

At the same time, it was also a wise move from the perspective of the bank's profitability and size. The move into previously unexplored markets produced huge numbers of new customers which ultimately increased Standard Trust Bank's bottom line. At a time when most other banks were still heavily focused on commercial interests, Tony saw the potential to be found in establishing a consumer base. The investors and stakeholders were delighted by the numbers; Tony was equally delighted by the fact that he was creating widespread social wealth, as well as financial gain for a few individuals.

With this increase in capital came further potential to widen their reach. By 2004, not only did they have branches all across Nigeria, they had also expanded across borders and commenced operations in neighboring Ghana. For a bank that had been on the brink of collapse in 1997, it was an astonishing feat. With a new focus on customer service and this aggressive expansion strategy into rural areas, Standard Trust Bank (STB) became one of the leading consumer banks, and the fifth largest in Nigeria, under Tony's leadership. And this was all achieved within a crowded market where there were over 120 operational banks at the time.

Alongside this expansion for their customers, Tony also worked on several major corporate and civil deals which had a significant impact on the Nigerian economy as a whole, solidifying both Tony and STB's importance in the nation's financial history. As a result, Tony transitioned from merely a young, successful CEO to an expert in his field. After Nigeria returned from military to democratic rule in 1999, he became a leading voice in economic development and an expert advisor to the ministers taking on their new roles. He helped to restructure the government's national debt and reduce this burden through innovative strategies. He also played an important part in the privatization of Nigerian Telecommunications Limited (NITEL) and the Nigerian Electric Power Authority (NEPA), coordinating the deals between stakeholders and agencies, and ultimately helping to improve the effectiveness and efficiency of these vital public services. Previously, they had been run inefficiently and with limited or inconsistent access to funding. By putting them out to tender and helping the best buyers from the private sector to secure the deal, Tony was instrumental in their improvement. Competition was encouraged in a way that ensured investment in *really* improving the infrastructure and outputs of these services was undertaken. It was a success for Tony's capitalist aims but also for the people of Nigeria who benefitted from better access to phone lines and electricity—two services that were fundamental to improving the life chances of people across the country and helping to draw communities out of poverty.

Once again, Tony's deep-seated belief in the importance of equal access to services and opportunities across the country had driven these deals. He saw the success of these deals as having a dual impact: He helped to improve the lives of millions of citizens, while at the same time creating capital in the economy that was vital to growing the nation's economy further. Philanthropy, it seems, was as much a calling for Tony as business and banking.

At the end of this transformative period of his career, from the lucky recipient of an entry-level job to the youngest branch manager and then the youngest CEO, Tony's youthful ambitions to become a well-dressed banker in his suspenders and brogues had also undergone a transformation. He had seen the power of finance and business to drive economic growth and real social change. He was now determined to become a leader in entrepreneurship—but also a champion for change in both Nigeria and Africa as a whole.

The Biggest Merger

Working alongside government ministers and helping to influence financial and economic policy gave Tony a unique insight into the future and further growth of the Nigerian banking sector. It allowed him to see—over and above his experience as the CEO of a single institution—the bigger picture and thus the gaps in the market into which he could potentially move.

Having established Standard Trust Bank as a leader among the newer institutions in the country and even successfully commenced operations in Ghana, Tony turned his attention to wider expansion and global reach. The final step of his plan was to take STB from the top 10 ranking of banks to the top 3. It was an ambitious aim, and yet, it was this vision which he had outlined from the very start of this journey, when first acquiring the distressed Crystal Bank, that had driven their expansion, determination, and success, propelling them to the position in the top 10.

Tony's 10-year strategy meant that there was always more to achieve on the horizon and more that could be done. Always looking ahead to the future created energy and innovation within the bank's management, and when they successfully achieved the first two stages of the plan, it made both the investors and employees even more determined to take the final leap. Seeing that their other aims were achievable, even when they had been labeled unrealistic or reckless by critics against the backdrop of an economic and political situation that continued to be unstable, gave Tony and STB a renewed sense of determination to accomplish everything they had set out to do.

Having breached the ranks of the top 10 in Nigeria, however, it was clear to Tony that Standard Trust Bank had reached something of a ceiling when it came to further growth, largely because it was such a new institution. Whilst their success with consumers had been second to none, the kind of growth that was needed to reach the highest echelons of the sector was reserved for the banks that had access to much larger reserves of capital, and longer-term relationships, than Standard Trust Bank. Thus, Tony knew that, in order to reach this final tier of his initial strategy, he would have to find a way to put these things within his reach. It was clear that STB would not be able to achieve this status on its own, and so, still well within the 10-year timeframe, Tony formulated another unique proposition: a merger with one of the oldest and most successful banks in Nigeria.

Just as he had carefully researched and chosen the right institution when he and his friends were ready to take over a bank, he patiently and diligently analyzed the potential options for this next move as well. This led him to approach the United Bank for Africa (UBA). At the time, the three banks operating consistently at the top of the leaderboard were First Bank, Union Bank, and UBA. UBA was actually the third most successful bank, not the first, but it was in this institution that Tony could see an alignment of vision, priorities, and thus, potential.

UBA had originally begun trading in 1949 as the British & French Bank (BFB), with UBA taking over these liabilities and becoming incorporated in 1961, just after independence. Already well-established before this seismic political change, it continued to prosper despite the struggles of the nation around it. UBA was the first Nigerian bank to make an initial public offering in 1970, listing its shares on the stock exchange in order to successfully raise a huge amount of capital for further investment. Branches in London and New York followed, turning UBA from a successful national venture into an international presence.

It was this influence and reach that Tony hoped to be able to utilize through the merger; he knew that, despite STB's meteoric rise, they couldn't access the same type of deals and success that UBA, with its long-standing reputation and more than 50-year history of financial stability, did. They had the dynamism of youth and the knowledge of how to run a successful bank for consumers, but they would never have the capacity that UBA, as such a trusted institution, had access to. Thus, he sought to find a way to acquire UBA's capacity, in this respect, for STB.

It took him two long years of negotiation, but one of the reasons that UBA had been such a strong institution over so many decades was the founders' belief, like Tony, in the importance of always looking and moving forward. They may have been one of the oldest banks in Nigeria, but they were not trapped in the past. Instead, they relished the opportunity for fresh ideas and strategies to raise fresh equity and drive further expansion. It was for these reasons that they were keen to merge with STB, even though it was a smaller and younger institution. In 2005, UBA took over another bank, Continental Trust, but in that same year, due to Tony's skillful negotiation, the deal with STB was a merger, not an acquisition; UBA wanted to integrate the dynamism and agility of this newer, younger model of finance into their established practices as a way to achieve further prosperity, rather than simply subsume its branches and assets.

The move put Tony at the heart of a historic moment again. In July 2005, the deal was complete. It was the biggest financial merger to have ever occurred in sub-Saharan Africa at the time. The media, having been charmed by Tony previously, followed the story with avid interest. This time, because so many citizens across Nigeria were the proud owners of an STB account, it was not just the financial newspapers and journalists who were interested—Tony had become the subject of major national news. He went from a household name solely within the banking sector to one of the most recognizable and admired businessmen in the country. Similarly, the merger itself was—and still is—widely reported on because it was so significant.

Integrating the values, working practices, and strategic intent of the two different parts of the bank was challenging at first. The two businesses used rival software programs, both with their own advantages and disadvantages. There were many choices that had to be made in regard to services, management, resources, and technology, all before the day-to-day running of the bank could operate smoothly. Getting staff from the two different institutions to work successfully alongside each other was also important, and Tony, typically, found innovative ways to foster team spirit and cooperation. For example, in making the decision about the software used, he tasked the teams from each bank to give a presentation on why one of the programs should be kept instead of the other. But the twist was that they had to sell the advantages of the program that had been used by the *other* bank, not the one used by themselves. It was a clever way to open lines of communication and remove any sense of proprietary or resentment over the final outcome.

The name was another important decision, and they considered whether to add the words "Standard Trust" to UBA in some capacity. But Tony had already seen the power of a name in his rebranding of the failing Crystal Bank, and so, the choice was taken to merge both banks under the umbrella of the brand "UBA Group," in order to bring the authority, tradition, and reputation that the UBA name conferred forward for the new institution. In each new challenge that the merger presented, Tony's ethos was thus: "Be humble, seek for advice, but be ready to make a decision" (*The History and Evolution of United Bank for Africa*, 2022). His ability and enthusiasm to discuss such important decisions with staff at all levels of management made him very popular with his employees. He was never afraid to ask for the opinions or advice of others in areas of their own expertise, never seeing it as a diminishment of his own knowledge or experience but instead appreciating the richness that different perspectives could provide. It also cemented the respect that the founders, investors, and board had for Tony because, despite his openness to discussion and debate, he was always decisive, even in the most challenging situations.

Tony and the founders of UBA were thus determined to overcome any differences in business culture or working practices quickly, and they were driven to do so by looking to the future once more. The merger made them the largest bank in Nigeria and solidified their influence in their home nation. When UBA Group officially commenced operations in August 2005, it became Nigeria's first mega-bank: It had 425 branches and offices, over 2 million active customers, and a balance sheet of more than 600 billion Naira (equivalent to $4.6 billion at the time). These impressive statistics were a strong foundation for Tony's new three-tier strategy. This time, his vision turned outwards, towards the rest of the continent. He now aimed to make UBA Group the top Pan-African bank, with branches spread throughout Africa and a strong presence in important centers for finance across the rest of the world.

In the years which followed, with Tony as the bank's CEO, integral in leading this strategic vision for UBA Group, just as he had been for Standard Trust Bank beforehand, UBA Group opened branches in Europe, in both London and Paris, and gained more than 7 million customers across 22 different African countries. Its presence across so much of Africa helped to make it a powerhouse in the banking sector, but also in commerce. UBA Group's reach and influence made it the bank of choice for many businesses operating or hoping to expand into other countries because it offered streamlined services across many borders. It also gave them the opportunity to play a significant role in public- and private-sector partnerships aimed at the development of the African markets. Furthermore, the establishment or expansion of branches of the UBA Group in New York, London, and Paris meant that the bank also played a leading role in accelerating the economic development of Africa abroad. African businesses which hoped to break into foreign markets, or international investors looking to take advantage of the potential in Africa, similarly found UBA Group to be their bank of choice. Once again, Tony accomplished the goal that he set out to achieve. UBA Group won a multitude of awards during this period, including taking the prestigious title of African Bank of the Year twice. They had become, as Tony had planned, the leading Pan-African bank.

His success during his tenure as CEO at UBA Group solidified him as one of the most important figures in banking in his country. But UBA Group was about more than just financial transactions: There was also an underlying mission to become a role model for African businesses. Tony wanted UBA Group to be known across the world for their professional and ethical standards and their outstanding leadership and enterprise. He transformed the banking sector in Nigeria in this way. UBA Group became an undisputed leader and dominant force in finance, but it was also enduring, honest, and principled. It demonstrated the importance of these qualities in an era plagued by accusations of corruption and moral bankruptcy.

However, the years in which Tony led the bank were not without their challenges. In 2006, the year after STB and UBA merged, Nigeria's financial sector was one of the fastest growing in the world—thanks in part to the advice given to the government by Tony and his peers, which led to changes in banking laws. But, in 2009, not long after the global financial crisis triggered by Wall Street the year before, the growth bubble burst. This resulted in many of the banks once again finding themselves in jeopardy when the stock market lost up to 70% of its value as oil prices—which were integral to Nigeria's economy—plunged rapidly. In a bid to protect the investments which had risen during the times of growth, the Central Bank provided capital to some of the ailing institutions, just as other governments around the world had done in 2008. But Nigeria also forcibly removed some managing directors who had failed to disclose bad loans, in contravention of the laws passed at the start of the decade, and who had arguably been partly to blame for the crash which occurred in their country. The Central Bank pushed for officials to be held to the same standard of professional and ethical practice and risk management that the UBA Group had successfully modeled—one of the few Nigerian banks not to face sanctions after the crash. The continuation of UBA Group's successful operation throughout this period of economic downturn must partly be attributed to Tony's high standards and commitment to transparent, ethical practices.

Although Tony stepped down as CEO in 2010, he later rejoined UBA Group as chairman of the board and has continued to support the bank in its constant innovation from this position. In his mission to bring economic opportunity to as many African citizens as possible and thus fuel the continent's development through business growth, Tony has forged relationships between organizations and entrepreneurs across Africa through the bank's investments. This has connected people and businesses through consumer, retail, and corporate banking, and UBA Group worked hard to reduce the bureaucracy and challenges of cross-border collaboration and trade through their Pan-African operations. The bank's diverse portfolio—established as a result of this exposure to such varied sectors and businesses across the continent—was another key factor in protecting them from the worst aftereffects of the economic crash in 2009, and this diversification continues to ensure that the bank and its investments remain healthy today.

Though Tony is no longer involved in the day-to-day operations and management of the bank, he remains crucial to its vision, drive, and reputation. It is Tony's long-standing belief in the importance of looking to the future, the potential for growth, and expansion which contributes to UBA Group's continued moves forward into new territories. In 2022, UBA Group became the first African bank to expand into the Gulf region when they were granted a license to operate in the United Arab Emirates. They remain an economic powerhouse as a result of this quest to diversify and expand, helping to connect Nigeria—and Africa, as a whole—with investment opportunities in different parts of the world. The opening of this branch in Dubai marks another step in their mission to develop the infrastructure and economy of Nigeria by helping the nation to establish a global presence on every continent and support African businesses in reaching the markets of the Middle East, just as they were so instrumental in doing through their American and European branches.

From Humble Beginnings

It is not just his bold, forward-thinking strategy that ensures that Tony remains the face of UBA Group today. It is also his confidence in narrating his own journey, and that of the bank, that makes him such a visible and recognizable figure; he exudes calm professionalism in front of any cameras. Thanks to his successes as CEO of Standard Trust Bank and the UBA Group, he has amassed a huge amount of personal wealth, but he also continues to be humble, unassuming, and respectful to all—another facet of his character that endears him to everyone who encounters him, whether in person, on television, or via the internet. Against the stunning backdrop of his sleek modern home, he is just as personable and charming to his audience as he was to his first customers and coworkers as a teller or entry-level analyst.

From his evenings huddled over his school books by the light of a kerosene lamp in his childhood home in Jos to meetings with financial heavyweights all over the world and a luxury home, Tony has journeyed an incredibly long way as a result of his banking career. For a dedicated young boy with relatively vague aspirations of being a businessman of an unspecified industry and a poor student with a desire to look good in suits, brogues, and suspenders, the breadth of Tony's influence as first the CEO and then the group chairman of the leading Pan-African bank would perhaps have been unimaginable, and yet, that is exactly what he has achieved.

Tony is always candid with interviewers about the role that he believes luck to have played in this truly remarkable journey, but the extent of his dedication, hard work, and tenacity should never be underestimated. His openness to constant innovation and drive to always look ahead to the future means that he has never been left behind by changes in the culture, technology, or fortunes of the financial industry. But these qualities have also kept him humble, despite the wealth and influence that he has accumulated: He is always willing to listen to the ideas of others and to promote those with talent; he has no fear of competition or being undermined, and his success has proved this to be a solid strategy.

Another important reason for Tony's continued humility is his wife, Dr Awele Vivien Elumelu, whom Tony married in 1993. Perhaps because they met when he was ambitious but still relatively unknown, Awele has long been a grounding, stable presence in Tony's life, as well as a reminder of the young dreamer that he used to be—the man who received a lucky chance from the chairman of AllStates Trust Bank when he was under-qualified for the position. This close tie to his past is one of the things that drives Tony's passion for helping young

Africans receive the same kind of opportunity and his desire to spread the luck which he remains grateful to have enjoyed himself. Ever the selfless, kind philanthropist, he wants to use his own good fortune to bolster that of others.

Despite their billion-dollar fortune, luxury home, and status in Nigeria, Tony and Awele live a fairly modest life. They are as dedicated to each other after 30 years of marriage as when they first met, and they guard their relationship closely from media scrutiny. They were both 30 years old when they got married and both young professionals at a similar stage in their careers. At the time that they met, Tony was a mid-career banker, and Awele was a doctor who had practiced medicine in Lagos and the UK. Both were well-educated and believed strongly in the power of schooling to change peoples' lives. They were from different parts of Nigeria and different backgrounds, yet their shared values and dreams were an integral part of their falling in love. From there, they grew together as a couple and as a family, and Awele has been an important champion for the youth and future of Africa, just like her husband.

Both Tony and Awele take their privacy, and that of their children, seriously, and they prefer to stay away from events and behavior that might feed the aura of celebrity around the family that Tony's success might otherwise garner. Although Tony is a regular figure on the national and global news or in the newspapers, he has carefully curated his image to ensure that the focus of interviews is always on his professional life rather than his personal one. The time he spends with his family is cherished and closely guarded.

Awele Elumelu is also an accomplished businesswoman in her own right, as well as a dedicated mother to the couple's seven children and a qualified doctor. However, she actively avoids the hype which she has often been the subject of. She hardly ever grants interviews and eschews social media, helping to keep the focus on Tony and what he can offer to the business world through his service and ideas, rather than allowing gossip or speculation to surround him. She has thus been quietly, confidently supportive of her husband throughout his career and an important reminder to Tony of what he values in the world.

Chapter 4:

Africapitalism

What Is Africapitalism?

Capitalism is a phenomenon that has been a major part of the philosophy and practice of economics in the Western world since the 18th century. After these societies underwent seismic social, cultural, and political change during the Industrial Revolution, and once the collapse of the ancient feudal systems was complete, capitalism became the prevailing economic system. It has dominated popular narratives and ideology ever since, particularly in the case of *The American Dream*, which underpinned the development of the United States of America. It also forms the basis for nearly all developed economies in the world today.

Fundamentally, it is an economic system in which individuals can own and control property and assets in accordance with their interests. This means that individuals are able to demand and set prices in a free market. The guiding principle behind this ownership and price setting is the motive to make a profit, and thus, the whole system is based on a transactional exchange of money. In a capitalist economy, therefore, labor is purchased for wages, capital gains on assets and businesses accrue to the owners, and prices allocate the monetary value of both the capital and labor against the competing demands of the economy.

However, whilst capitalism has been the driving force in the Western world, where it is able to take advantage of preexisting economies of scale, innovation, and institutional settings, this has not been the case in Africa because of the underlying social and cultural challenges. Free markets can only flourish when the conditions and rules—often established by government intervention and policy—allow them to.

It was against this backdrop that, in 2011, Tony Elumelu first coined the term "Africapitalism." In his capacity as CEO of Standard Trust Bank and then UBA Group, Tony furthered both his academic and practical understanding of economics. He worked closely alongside business leaders and policymakers in his own country, but he also traveled widely to oversee operations at UBA Group's branches in the West. The more that he witnessed firsthand, and the more journals and studies published by both African and Western universities that he read, the more he became convinced that Africa needed its own, unique set of ideas, rules, and guidelines to achieve comparable economic success. He could see, through his experiences and relationships, that Africa had huge potential, but also that it was so fundamentally different from America, England, France, and other developed nations that applying concepts that had previously existed wouldn't work. He was also aware of the contemporary nature of Africa's struggles to define and improve itself, and he was becoming increasingly frustrated to find that many academics, economists, and politicians were trying to apply or utilize traditional capitalist ideas from previous centuries in this modern, complex context. No wonder, Tony started to realize, so many ventures had been unsuccessful.

It was one morning, just after he had returned from one such trip abroad, that Tony found himself brooding on this concept at his home.

Having said goodbye to his children as they headed off to school, he felt uncharacteristically demotivated and did not immediately head to either his office upstairs or the bank headquarters, as he would usually do after a period away. Instead, he wandered the wide corridors of his house, a second cup of coffee in his hand, feeling restless and discontented. He paused in front of the glossy white bookcases in the family room, the colors of book spines catching his eye from between the framed family photographs and the trinkets and treasures that his wife had so beautifully curated on the shelves. There was a diverse range of fiction, non-fiction, and children's literature arranged along the full width of the room, although many of the larger, weightier volumes belonged to Tony's personal collection and so tended to be focused on business and economics.

As he ran his fingers down some of their glossy spines, he was struck again by the sense that much of the theory of business that already existed was not fit for purpose. The various titles did not seem to encapsulate the unique challenges and opportunities for Africa and capitalism that he knew existed. There needed to be an explanation and ideology of how they could be combined. It was then that the name came to Tony's mind: Africapitalism.

Suddenly energized, Tony abandoned his half-drunk coffee on the table and raced upstairs to his home office. He seized a pen and wrote fervently, ideas pouring from his mind onto the paper in a wave of inspiration. It was as if they had been waiting to be released. He barely registered the sounds of the phone ringing or his wife downstairs. Emails went unanswered. He was so consumed with the task of bringing his thoughts to life. At last, having outlined his ideas in as much detail as he could, he looked up from his desk, realizing that the sun was low in the sky, signaling that evening was approaching outside the window and that he had spent most of the day working in a feverish passion. He gathered the pages together, feeling dazed, and went to share them with his wife before the children came home from school. If she was surprised to see him emerge from his office, clutching a stack of writing to his chest, having previously been so silent and uncommunicative all day, she did not say so. But when she read through the beginning of his proposals, he could tell by the look on her face that she knew that what he had written was every bit as important as he had thought.

Since its inception, Africapitalism has gained traction on a global stage in both business and academic settings. It is an acknowledgment that, although capitalism does not fundamentally alter its basic shape and ideology in different regions of the world, it does encounter different circumstances, challenges, and opportunities in each of these regions. Thus, it argues, the model of capitalism which should be applied, in practice, to Africa should be unique to the conditions on the ground in Africa itself. Once he had begun to share his ideas with coworkers and peers, Tony realized from their responses that he had created something that had the power to exceed the models that already existed in the Western world and thus create an ideology and system which really benefited Africa and its people in the future.

But what actually is Africapitalism? Firstly, it is important to establish that it is a philosophy that has always underpinned Tony's approach to business and the world as a whole. When he sat down to set out his vision for Africapitalism, he was, in many ways, merely giving a concrete shape to the beliefs that he had always held and demonstrated in his career up until that point. Another fundamental part of understanding this term is to see the importance that it ascribes to Africa, when the continent had previously been left out of such philosophical conversations because they had traditionally been dominated by ideas and narratives formed in the northern half of the Western hemisphere. Tony gave a voice and legitimacy to an Africa-centric approach that recognized and celebrated the differences between the continent and traditional capitalist economies, rather than trying to downplay or overlook them. He also brought international attention to the need to change the way that the global community viewed Africa's place in the modern world. For far too many decades, the strategy and mindset towards development had been focused on the same methods and delivery, without considering how much Africa had already changed or its huge future potential.

But Tony's treatise redefined Africa's private sector as the key to the continent's development—not just public services and infrastructure or international aid, which had historically been the vehicles used through which to promote growth. As his philosophy was shared eagerly across Africa and beyond, Africapitalism began to chip away at this fixed mindset. The more exposure that these ideas received, and the more they appeared in important publications like *The Economist*, the more Tony marveled at the power of ideas to change the world.

At the heart of it all, when Tony was feverishly writing his first draft of his research paper, he was envisioning a future that was made by Africa, for Africa. His statement outlined a clear path to prosperity and wealth, rebranding Africa as a place of investment, innovation, and entrepreneurship rather than poverty—of business and progress rather than charity. There are eight fundamental principles that underpin the philosophy, the first of which is entrepreneurship.

Entrepreneurship

Tony has always believed in the power of business to create economic growth and prosperity, but he also places great stake in the ability of individuals to drive this type of change and growth. In many ways, he is an important example of such success himself, as time and again throughout his career, it was him, as an individual, who was the recipient of the trust, belief, and investment of others.

Tony's first principle of Africapitalism involves unlocking this potential across the continent's youth, helping to create opportunities for these individuals to fuel economic development and investment potential. He asserts that this path forward is unique to Africa, its demographic, and its emerging capitalist market. In contrast to China, where state-run enterprise fuels the economy, and Korea's huge conglomerates or India's family-run businesses, the model of Africapitalism sees individual innovation and creativity as the way to build prosperity.

But Tony doesn't see the private sector as solely responsible for driving this time of future and potential: He believes that investment in entrepreneurship should come from all sources, including public and philanthropic funds. Instead of traditional types of aid, he believes that a model of investing in entrepreneurs should be adopted by both global and African philanthropists as a way to stimulate the rise of Africapitalism. He cites the way that some philanthropic agencies and NGOs have already begun to make an impact in this respect; experiments in channeling development funding into entrepreneurial investments have already proven to be successful in providing handsome returns, as well as creating wealth in other strata of society.

Longer-Term Investments

Just as he did when he took over the failing Crystal Bank, Tony continues to understand the importance of waiting for assets to grow over time, rather than focusing on a fast return on a principal sum. Africapitalism is about having that long-term vision because patience is what will ultimately grow real value. This is why Tony's banking career was always driven by three-tier strategies: He was investing in the long-term future, looking ten years or more ahead, rather than just at the next profit margin.

Tony also hopes to see a change in mindset around the oil and mining industries, which are still such an integral part of the economy in Nigeria and many other African nations because of their focus on the hasty extraction of resources from the soil and a fast return, rather than considering the long-term impact and potential. Tony cites the Nigerian oil industry as a prime example: They have been producing crude oil and natural gas for export since the 1950s, yet Nigeria still has to import refined petroleum for its own consumption.

It is this type of behavior—a "rent-seeking" mindset in Tony's philosophy, which encourages businesses to focus on expending resources to capture a higher share of the existing wealth—that has historically dominated the private sector in Africa. As these methods do not actually create new wealth or thus drive future growth, Africapitalism instead focuses on seeking profit by creating new economic and social wealth. By breaking free of the compulsion to exploit and extract wealth from the ground or the labor market in the old ways, growth and development can become much more sustainable in the long term since they also have fewer boundaries and limits on their potential.

Strategic Sectors

Tony's vision for overall growth and future prosperity similarly includes a call to recognize the importance of investing in a broad portfolio that supports each nation. As well as just investing in certain businesses or sectors that are already performing well and could deliver a strong financial return, he advocates for a more philanthropic and service-based approach where those who are able to also invest in infrastructure or businesses with more of a social or national value, rather than just those with the fastest return.

This is how he believes agriculture, healthcare, and power will be able to thrive. They can be less attractive prospects, yet improving these strategic sectors could have a dramatic impact on the wealth of a nation overall, thus helping to improve the profitability and prosperity of other industries as a result and delivering a return that comes full circle for the investors in the end.

This investment in strategic sectors is a strategy that Tony demonstrated could be successful during his leadership of Standard Trust Bank, where his expansion into the consumer and retail market was of huge benefit not only to the bank but also to the customers who were provided with services they previously did not have access to. He could have chosen to follow a different, arguably easier, path with the bank, yet he deliberately followed one which had social value as well. Other investors should be encouraged to make similarly moral and responsible choices in their strategy.

Development Dividends

On the other side of the coin, Tony envisions these sectors changing the way that they issue financial returns for shareholders to ensure that investment is ongoing. Although social and economic benefit is vital for nations, he understands that development and growth won't be possible without the ongoing interest of financiers and that incentives are the key to encouraging the long-term and strategic investments needed to actually fuel development over time. There should not be a reliance on goodwill or philanthropy; the investments in these sectors need to provide a profitable return in order to continue to stimulate this strategy.

Thus, market liberalization and government reform must create the circumstances in which it is in the interests of capitalists to adopt the strategy of Africapitalism and pursue these types of ventures. Fundamentally, entrepreneurs, capitalists, and multinational companies do not invest out of altruism. Businesses and markets are created out of a competition for capital and relative opportunity, seeking a return that is commensurate with the risks that are taken. By creating the conditions in which entrepreneurial value and social or national wealth creation are prioritized and attractive, the strongest returns can be provided and encourage further investment in a virtuous cycle.

Value-Added Growth

Tony further understands the need to work with what is most widely available in a local area to ensure the highest value of results. Nigeria— and, of course, the continent as a whole—is a vast, broad area, and this can create challenges around supply chains or expenses, leaving some businesses or investments to become less profitable in certain regions as a result. Tony believes in leveraging the capital, workers, and raw materials that already exist locally, as this will create a higher value of growth overall.

This also reflects back on the need for longer-term investments and investment into the right kind of sectors and strategies. Though there has been significant economic growth in Africa since the year 2000, Tony reports that much of it is neither valuable nor sustainable because it has been created by the export of resources. He acknowledges that there has been a gain in GDP because of the profit and money coming into the continent in return for the resources which leave but confirms that this has not actually added any value to the community and economies in the long term. Unemployment has seen little reduction during the same period, despite the increase in GDP, because this type of growth does not fuel the creation of jobs and social wealth in its wake. Africapitalism, in contrast, advocates for an approach that leads to both GDP growth and employment. Instead of these short-term, "rent-seeking" enterprises that often leave communities worse off,

Tony's approach involves building up opportunities to emerge from poverty and solving the problems within those communities—all at the same time as delivering returns to businesses.

A key example of this, which Tony is a staunch supporter of, is agriculture. Agribusiness can generate a return on investment, but he also draws attention to the way that it addresses two of Africa's most critical problems: food scarcity and rural unemployment. There are vast tracts of land across the continent that have the potential to be arable, but investment has not been forthcoming in this area because the focus has historically been on exportation instead. Despite the space that Africa has at its disposal, the continent is actually a net food importer, and this contributes to the recurrent issues around food security. Because investment has continued to be poor in this sector, the resulting lack of technology and entrepreneurship plaguing the world of agriculture means that farm yields in much of Africa are among the lowest in the world. Even when the yields are higher, the poor infrastructure, few domestic processing facilities, and lack of adequate storage mean that a high percentage of the crops which are produced end up being wasted. Thus, there is huge potential here for value-added growth: Agriculture could be Africa's biggest economic success story with the right investment, Tony argues, because it has such potential for value-added growth.

Regional Connectivity

However, a challenge that then arises from this strategy of encouraging local specialisms to thrive in this way is how to create supply chains across the huge geographical expanses. Tony's next proposal of Africapitalism, therefore, centers on improving regional connectivity and the importance of creating robust supply chains since those that are longer, better integrated, and of higher value would help to facilitate interregional and Pan-African trade as a whole. Not only does Tony believe in the importance of developing national infrastructure to support growth and development, he also understands the importance of cross-border commerce and trade. For this to be a success, policies, practices, and bureaucracy need to be streamlined in order to create an attractive prospect to businesses and investors. This is one of the reasons why he continues to push for the expansion of UBA Group in Africa and beyond, to a global scale, in his capacity as chairman—to manufacture these connections and reduce the obstacles which might otherwise discourage business owners from operating across borders.

When intra-African trade happens, Tony emphasizes, there is a greater impact on both the wider economy and society than when trade occurs with companies outside of Africa. This is because when Africa is both the primary driver and beneficiary of the trade, the rewards are more than just monetary: It encourages future investment and growth, as well as more sustainable employment and domestic infrastructure. Furthermore, it encourages the integration of Africa's diverse communities and becomes a way to share best practices in business and create domestic talent, rather than encouraging the exportation of resources or the economic migration of the skilled workforce.

Multigenerational Development

Even as he grows older and wiser, Tony continues to focus his sights on the youth of Africa. He knows how young, hardworking, and hungry he was when he was first starting out and sees how unlocking that potential will be another key to Africa's development. This belief is a direct result of his successes as a young man whose mentors believed in him. But it is also fuelled by a much wider understanding of the continent as a whole. Nigeria has a young population, as does much of Africa, unlike most Western countries.

Prioritizing African youths is, therefore, about more than common sense for future expansion: Too many feel disenfranchised and isolated by the lack of employment opportunities and the bleak vision of the future they envisage for themselves in such a crowded market, so they must be reengaged in working to build the type of world that they want to live in. Thus, Tony proposes that investment and development should be focused on creating a robust future that properly considers the needs, wants, and skills of the largest demographic in Africa in order to stop so many young people from migrating abroad and effectively creating a "brain drain" of talent which, in turn, has an increasingly negative impact on long-term growth.

Shared Purpose

In addition to creating strong relationships across borders and generations, Africapitalism also advocates for collaboration between different stakeholders, from government ministers to academics to philanthropists. Tony proposes that they all need to work together to create the kind of social, economic, and cultural conditions in which young entrepreneurs can actually thrive. Seeing and believing in a shared purpose will empower the private sector to succeed further, just as each of Tony's victories throughout the stages of his three-tier strategic plans helped to fuel his own determination and drive in his banking career, as well as his employees and peers.

This final principle that underpins Africapitalism also embodies Tony's acknowledgment of the way that capitalism often has quite a narrow, limited definition that does not consider the breadth and scope of its own potential in different regions of the world. Although capitalism is fundamentally about wealth creation and profit, Tony highlights the fact that it could also offer an unparalleled opportunity to improve social conditions as well. Yet, businesses have historically been overlooked as vehicles to provide this social wealth in Africa because of the tendency to favor a model which has relied on charitable donations or public services instead. Social improvement and economic value have typically been seen as oppositional, rather than complementary, and thus, the potential for business growth to share the purpose and goals of social development has often been ignored.

But Tony's philosophy of Africapitalism looks past this, expanding the definitions of a "market" and "value" to include societal needs as well as economic ones. Creating value for society ultimately fuels value for the business, he argues, just as causing societal harm inevitably creates problems and costs for businesses as well. Understanding the importance of shared values can promote a cycle in which companies and communities prosper alongside each other, as well as mitigating the potential for the costs and negative impact on both businesses and society that comes from working in opposition to each other. It is, after all, in the capital owners' interest to consider social impact because this will create more profit in the long run—which is ultimately the goal of capitalism.

A Call to Action

Africapitalism is actually quite a simple notion at its heart—Tony is emphasizing that the private sector must be involved in national development, not just the government agencies and philanthropic international organizations which have been relied on in the past. Yet, despite this underlying simplicity, it is also a powerful, even radical, vision that could remake the continent and put it on a par with capitalist Western nations if the mindset of both Nigeria and the global business world as a whole can be changed to support it.

African countries are still mostly classed as "developing nations," and so, they are, in effect, the final frontier in terms of capitalist expansion and growth. Thus, Africapitalism proposes that a change in fortune for this content could offer real opportunities for global economic evolution and expansion: Some markets in Africa are untapped sources of income, and there are both human and natural resources just waiting to be used if the support of the right infrastructure and expertise can be forthcoming. Though many of the large capitalist economies in the West have slowed or stagnated in the years since the 2008 financial crash, Africa, by contrast, offers boundless opportunities for the future. Investing in Africa is not about goodwill or charity; the potential for return is real. The burgeoning private sector is already proof of this, and Tony is a prime example of how domestic companies can thrive in this environment. UBA Group has over 7 million customers, 20,000 employees, and banks in more than 20 countries, and their investors have seen significant returns as a result.

However, Africapitalism is not just about building businesses. Tony also envisions that economic growth is the key to solving the social challenges that continue to plague the continent. Social wealth can potentially go hand in hand with commercial objectives because private-sector development actually has the potential to improve self-sufficiency and infrastructure in a more powerful way than charities or international aid can offer. The prosperity and opportunities created by a long-term, stable employer in a particular region or rural area are twofold: This brings wealth to families and employees in the short-term, but it also necessitates an improvement in healthcare, education, and other sectors in order to sustain a reliable workforce. Other businesses and services also typically spring up as a result, complementing or competing with the opportunities created by the first organization. This becomes a sustainable and generative cycle that can only grow stronger. Moreover, the prospect of paid employment is a powerful tool for motivation and inspiration, the importance of which must not be underestimated in the journey out of extreme poverty and social problems.

In contrast, continuing aid can help to support a community on a limited basis, but it cannot create a sustainable future, no matter how well-intentioned and well-planned the assistance is. When the aid is reduced or removed, the road out of the problems that the community faces is blocked off once again. Similarly, an overreliance on aid creates a fixed mindset in both international investors and local citizens so that they fail to see the potential that the area holds. Africapitalism is, however, fundamentally based on change, growth, and independence.

Socialism—the major competing economic system and philosophy in the world today—is often seen as the primary way to create social change because the state owns the means of production and thus seeks to improve social good through enterprise, rather than working towards profits for individuals. Yet, because of the historical instability in governments and regimes, creating public or state ownership of all resources and services isn't really a viable option for much of Africa. This is why Tony believes Africapitalism can fill this gap between socialism and traditional capitalism; although capitalism is founded on the concept of self-interest and the pursuit of individual wealth through profit, without regard for sociopolitical motives, in practice, he feels that it can benefit society too. He partly attributes this to the fundamental importance of competition in the system. Businesses have the freedom to enter or exit a market, and interactions between buyers and sellers determine the prices of goods, services, and wages. Essentially, when competition between companies exists, consumers have the freedom to choose which goods and services to buy, and workers can leave their jobs for better pay or improved working conditions. Return on investment and the market itself are driven by consumption and production, but only for those goods, services, and jobs which offer the highest reward. Such healthy levels of competition, Tony believes, can ultimately help communities to thrive by offering decent remuneration for employment and quality goods and services, rather than a reliance on state-owned or managed enterprises which are only able to pay a fixed amount or provide a certain, often limited, service. Thus, he proposes that, in Africa, the success and wealth of a few individuals can actually contribute to overall prosperity because the markets are ready and waiting for such opportunities.

Tony Elumelu's success in the banking sector in Nigeria is an important example of this in action—and the reason why he has such a deep-seated personal belief in this philosophy. When he acquired the distressed Crystal Bank in 1997, he implemented a service that was of benefit to the community as part of his strategy. This was many years before he had considered the concept of Africapitalism, but you can see that the ideas that underpin it have always been at the heart of Tony's vision. When the bank was on the brink of collapse, threatening investors' capital and also the jobs of many workers, he was able to turn it around and give the bank a new lease of life, when others may have supported the liquidation of its assets as the easier path. Whilst the bank's survival under the rebranded Standard Trust Bank name protected those jobs and investments, there was also another part of this venture that had a much wider social function that exemplifies the strategic, value-added growth proposed by Africapitalism.

Through their policy of expansion outside of the Lagos area and Tony's commitment to widening the equality of opportunity in financial services, they effectively democratized banking in Nigeria. The expansion was a tried and tested business practice: They grew their customer base, improved the stability and health of the bank, and delivered significant returns, all of which benefited the individuals at the heart of the rebranded bank, such as Tony himself. Yet, many others benefitted too. At the time, there were over 110 million citizens in Nigeria, yet fewer than 10% had bank accounts—a tiny fraction of the population. Tony tapped into this unrealized potential and unmet demand. In doing so, he was enacting the principles that guide Africapitalism, before its inception: By improving the business prospects and profitability of the bank through this strategy, he also improved the prospects of many other Nigerians at the same time. They did not make these moves without regard for profit or as a result of goodwill, yet there was, simultaneously, a profound social effect.

The hundreds of branches they opened increased access to these services, solving systemic problems, eliminating inefficiencies, and improving productivity among consumers.

Later, Standard Trust Bank also became the first large-scale bank to offer online services, embracing technological advances to improve their customers' experiences, as well as innovate their practices. For example, parents of children who attended school in different states and lived away from home no longer had to travel across the country in order to give their children some money or pay their school fees; they were able to use online banking or visit a branch much closer to their home. In this way, personal finance and transactions like these could be managed from home or an office, saving time, money, and effort for Standard Trust Bank's clients. When these additional functions for their bank accounts came into effect, the swift rise in demand and the popularity of STB's accounts spoke volumes about how important this unmet need was in many communities and the sincere impact that it had on their daily lives. STB became a symbol of a new, energized Nigeria and the rise of a culture that understood the importance of looking forward to the future to find ways to improve the sustainability and self-sufficiency of the community in the long term.

It was for these reasons that Tony found himself outlining the principles of Africapitalism: He wanted to empower domestic businesses, and international investors alike, to create a culture in which other companies could see the benefits of the same types of investments and strategies that he himself had successfully followed in the financial sector. The term "Africapitalism" itself, and the paper he published, were therefore intended to be a call to action for entrepreneurs everywhere: a way to change the fixed mindsets that perceived Africa as a place of charity, rather than a sound investment for the future.

It is his mission to convince the world to make the decision to invest in Africa and its potential for economic growth whilst many of the Western capitalist economies experience downturns in fortune. And alongside the economic wealth which will be created as a result of this investment, Tony believes that social wealth and development could also be promoted at the same time, with communities becoming better-educated, more skilled, and thus, better employees. These employees may even become entrepreneurs who work alongside their former employers, using the experience gained in their local area to start their own businesses which meet the needs of the local community or find a way to utilize the strengths of their region.

Africapitalism is, essentially, a vision of self-empowerment for the continent of Africa. Tony created this philosophy because he understands that the focus, rationale, and strategy of investment need to change in today's modern Africa. And this is because the nature of the opportunity has changed after decades of fluctuation and development. Africa is not the place that it was at the start or end of colonial rule; it is not even the same place that it was at the start of the new millennium. Thus, he argues, these changes must be advocated for, both in Africa and on the global stage.

Tony's first call to action concerns the perception of Africa as a place that is not fit for business. Based on the population growth and demographic trends—both of which prove that Africa has the most youthful, dynamic workforce on the planet—it is actually one of the most attractive prospects for investment. Much of the world, however, is still hung up on the concerns and stereotypes of the past. The young population of Africa are ambitious, focused on change, hardworking, and driven. They are determined to break away from the challenges of the past, but preconceptions and prejudices continue to stop businesses and investors from seeing how much the youthful workforce could offer them. This is one of the problems that Tony hopes the concept of Africapitalism will change because Africa's markets are actually growing rapidly alongside its population. Not only is there a huge pool of labor to assist in the continent's development, there has also been a rapid growth in the number of consumer groups and new customer bases with spending power. Meeting the demands of Africa's youthful demographic has huge potential in a wide range of sectors, as long as businesses can stop seeing Africa in an outdated way. And the time for action is now: By 2040, Africa will be home to 20% of the world's workforce and, thus, also its consumers (Elumelu, 2011). This statistic brings a real imperative to Tony's theory. If the world cannot change the way it perceives Africa before this becomes a reality, the potential will not be able to be fully realized.

Moreover, the old-fashioned ideas and preponderance of narratives about Africa being a place of charity, not business, ignores the economic growth that has happened there over the past decade. Recently, reforms in regulation, transparency, and law have been accelerating, removing many of the barriers to capitalist development which previously existed. Yet, Africa is still seen as unprepared for development because of the persistent nature of these historical stereotypes. It is certainly true that obstacles to growth remain in Africa—particularly poor infrastructure and cumbersome public or regulatory bodies and bureaucratic processes—but such challenges can only be overturned in the long term by the development of the economy in spite of these obstacles. In essence, Africapitalism can create a virtuous cycle: Investment and business growth helps to draw attention to where the issues and inconveniences remain, pushing further reform. This, in turn, improves the conditions in which businesses can operate, leaving the door open for more entrepreneurship and further reform as a result. It has already been proven possible by those African and international companies who have persevered and been committed to overcoming these obstacles: They have prospered as a result.

Many of the governments which were first established after independence from colonial rule, including in Nigeria, often managed industries centrally and regulated markets in an attempt to stabilize or boost economic growth. But several decades after this period of transition, this is no longer the case. As nations have begun to navigate the challenges of democracy more successfully, the old model of public management and control of enterprise has gradually been reduced, paving the way for free markets and businesses to flourish. African nations have begun to realize that they are not responsible for actually running industries or businesses via their governments. Instead, they understand that their responsibilities lie in providing a supportive and structured environment in which businesses can thrive, with ease, safety, and transparency at its heart.

As a whole, the markets are becoming fairer, more transparent, and more open as a result of these advancements in both government policies and private enterprise. Whilst there is still a tendency within the African private sector towards short-term "rent-seeking" ventures that yield a fast profit and extraction of existing wealth, the recent improvements to the conditions and practice of business in Africa are still vast. If governments can change their policies to encourage Africapitalism's guiding principles through systemic, political change, Tony believes that the tendency to engage in this kind of short-term thinking can be overcome and the focus shifted to the creation of new wealth instead. With the rapid evolution of Africa's markets and consumer groups, companies must build brands and customer bases to fully realize their potential and continually reinvest to fuel growth. This is a forward-thinking model of business which completely contrasts the old reliance on governments to manage or encourage the markets, rather than the businesses and investors themselves.

Nowadays, with the private sector ready, waiting, and open to investment and reinvigoration, Tony's mission is to overturn all of these preconceptions of Africa and thus help investors to understand this potential. He calls on entrepreneurs in Africa, as well as foreign and domestic investors, to be forward-thinking and embrace the opportunities currently on offer. He wants to create momentum in the economic development of Africa—to seek out growth and thus create more growth in a way that will deliver value and success for all. He also calls on NGOs and African governments to work together with the private sector and establish a partnership with them that will fuel real social and economic change in the long term. He exhorts them to join the campaign by supporting the ingenuity and innovation that the private sector can offer. He asks for them to create an environment that enables capitalism to flourish—to act as regulators and governors, not as controllers or instigators.

But Tony also calls on Africans themselves to embrace his philosophy. Rather than relying on exports and quick returns, they need to build the kinds of companies that have a real future in Africa and can create real benefits within the continent. They must make the kind of products that new consumer groups in Africa actually want to buy, rather than importing them. They must take ownership of the manufacturing process, rather than allowing multinational companies to control the industry and funnel the profits back into other economies overseas. They must take advantage of the workforce and opportunities that are available to them and create companies that utilize this to the advantage of both profit and social change. They must create businesses that fit the unique context and circumstances of Africa to truly build a capital base. Africans must lead by example, investing in domestic industry and businesses to establish their place in the world. They cannot simply wait for outsiders or international investors to make the first move.

As a result of strong partnerships between businesses, investors, governments, charities, and individuals, Africa can accomplish all these things. It will be the collective impact that ultimately produces the most successful results. With such huge population growth and change already occurring, rapid action toward these goals must happen now. Africa must act now to meet the demands of its future on its own terms; otherwise, it risks being overtaken by events instead.

Although Africa has seen some growth since the start of the 21st century, Africapitalism is vital to its future. Without it, Africa has failed to make enough gains in value and wealth creation over the past two decades to compete with the growth of other continents. It is still the case that too many consumer goods are purchased from abroad and that the economy still relies too heavily on exporting resources. The continent that is seen as underdeveloped has, in truth, been overexploited by those outside its borders, and Africans themselves must aim to create the real, long-term economic growth that will ultimately allow Africa to become self-sufficient.

It was in May 2014, at the World Economic Forum (WEF) in Abuja, that Tony formally launched his call to action with the announcement of the establishment of the Africapitalism Institute. Like many entrepreneurs, Tony had long been an admirer of the World Economic Forum and its mission to shape global and regional economic agendas to find solutions to some of the world's most pressing issues. The WEF's belief in the importance of public-private cooperation so closely aligned with the philosophy of Africapitalism that he knew a WEF regional event would be the ideal opportunity to launch the Institute and deliver his call to action to the world.

In a leafy area of central Abuja stands the Transcorp Hilton Hotel, a luxury hotel with views over Millennium Park and the golden roof of the National Mosque. Located near many government offices and major corporate headquarters, it was the perfect place to host the first WEF event in the new Nigerian capital to discuss business and political issues, and solutions, in Africa. Within the hotel's extensive conference facilities, Tony explained his plan for the Africapitalism Institute to a room of executives, leaders, influential thinkers, and journalists. It was to be the first Pan-African think tank headquartered, founded, and funded by Africans, and the world was excited to hear what Tony had to say.

At the press conference, alongside the other esteemed members of the panel, including the President of the African Development Bank, the Administrator of the United States Agency for International Development, and David Rice, the Director of the Institute, Tony explained the importance of the move to those assembled. He described the need to promote the principles of Africapitalism through the Institute in order to encourage the private sector to embrace these ideas and the way that the training and support it would provide would help entrepreneurs and leaders commit to building sustainable, socially responsible businesses in Africa. He also listed the organizations and institutions that would be working in partnership with them, including the representatives seated beside him at the microphones in the front of the meeting room. They would help the Institute to conduct research and advocacy, spreading Tony's message and promoting inclusive economic growth across the continent.

"The Africapitalism Institute belongs to all of us," Tony told the crowd. "It will focus on academically rigorous, practically applicable research and multi-stakeholder engagement to advocate for public policies and business practices that will unlock opportunities for all Africans" (*The Tony Elumelu Foundation launches Africapitalism Institute*, 2014).

Heirs Holdings

In 2010, when Tony stepped down from the role of CEO at UBA Group, it was not to step back from the world of commerce or the influence that he wielded in Nigeria as a result of his successes and notoriety in that role. Instead, he was looking to expand both his experience in business beyond finance and his capacity to serve his nation beyond the realm of these services. Thus, Heirs Holdings was created: a family-run company that invests in a wide range of different sectors across Africa.

Their diverse portfolio includes the power, oil, and gas industries, hospitality, real estate, healthcare, and finance. The companies they invest in operate in 24 different countries across the world. They now have over 600 employees. But Heirs Holdings, as you might expect with Tony at the helm, is much more than just a profitable investment holding company in Nigeria.

There is one fundamental aim and belief that underpins all of their investment decisions and the company's values: Africapitalism. From the very beginning of the company, the moves they made were intended to enable social wealth as well as profit for their shareholders. In essence, Heirs Holdings seeks to put the principles and call to action of Africapitalism into practice. Once Tony had formally put pen to paper and shared his vision of Africapitalism with the media and the world, Heirs Holdings became a model and guiding light to other investors, both in Africa and across the globe. They aim, in partnership with other groups, to invest in markets and industries that can have a real effect on the long-term creation of wealth and thus contribute to holistic development in Africa, at the same time providing a profit and return on investment for Heirs Holdings themselves.

In a move that was as bold, confident, and determined as those that characterized his earlier career in banking, Tony's first strategy was to acquire a controlling stake in Nigeria's largest listed conglomerate. In 2011, Transcorp's business interests spanned multiple sectors, including energy, agriculture, and hospitality—including the iconic Transcorp Hilton Hotel in the capital city. Yet, despite the fact that Transcorp had a very large, loyal shareholder base and had stakes in companies in some of the most promising industries and firms in the country, they had been consistently underperforming. It was these disappointing returns and their lack of forward-thinking that inspired Tony to seek out a controlling stake in such an infamous company, even though it was his first major investment opportunity. He employed the same vision and self-belief that had led him to become the youngest branch manager and then the youngest CEO at the time, and once again, his gamble paid off. Transcorp benefitted hugely from the skill, knowledge, and expertise that Tony and his coworkers at Heirs Holdings brought to the deal. Soon, it had been transformed into a prosperous corporation, just as Tony had hoped. It was a brilliant start to the next stage of his career as an investor.

Similarly, just as his three-tier strategy for the new Standard Trust Bank had been ambitious enough to expand across the whole continent and led to the largest financial merger in sub-Saharan Africa with UBA Group, Tony wanted to achieve the same reach and impact with Heirs Holdings. During the first year of operations, they successfully made their first impact investment outside of Nigeria, which showed their determination to play a leading role in economic and social development across as much of the continent as possible. This first Pan-African joint investment was in Mtanga Farms in Tanzania, an arable business focused on potato production in the East African region. The business used seed potatoes from a new variety of potatoes to improve the yield and thus the income of the smallholding farmers. This initiative increased the wealth of the individual farmers and their communities, but it also had a significant effect on wider economic development by boosting the productivity and profitability of the farmers. It created more employment, provided food security, supported the retail sector, and generally contributed to the economic development of the area in this way.

Furthermore, in 2013, Heirs Holdings committed the largest amount from a single private investor in the Power Africa Initiative led by Barack Obama. They pledged 2.5 billion American dollars to support the scheme's ambition to vastly increase the capacity and generation of electricity in sub-Saharan Africa. This is another prime example of Africapitalism in action: Heirs Holdings leading a scheme backed by international supporters on the front line in Africa, making their own profit in the long term by providing energy, simultaneously improving the lives and chances of millions of citizens. Via Transcorp, Heirs Holdings had acquired Ughelli Power PLC—the largest electric power plant in Nigeria—in 2013, when it was privatized by the government, and thus, the investment group had both the expertise and infrastructure in place to make these kinds of changes happen. By 2018, Transcorp Power had surpassed the five-year performance targets that had been set for them within a four-year period, demonstrating that performance, profitability, and social wealth can go hand in hand. The Power Africa Initiative is exactly the kind of scheme that Tony envisioned in 2010 when he first coined the term "Africapitalism" and is a clear demonstration of both the ability and importance of the private sector's impact on poverty.

Tony's decision to step down from UBA Group as the CEO after 10 years of running the bank gave him the chance to show just how powerful these types of investments in the private sector could be in Africa. As he continues to grow his reputation and professional relationships across the globe, Tony proves how the concept of Africapitalism could transform millions of lives. Although Tony Elumelu and Heirs Holdings remain at the heart of Africapitalism, it now arguably transcends Tony and his own investments. As the idea has gained more and more traction among both African investors and the global business community, and as the world has seen its success being put into practice, it has gained a life of its own. Although not all entrepreneurs in Africa believe in it, it has certainly managed to create an emotive force and sense of momentum among them over the past decade. It has helped to provide a roadmap towards economic prosperity, even if there are still many challenges and inequalities to overcome on the way to the final destination of success.

Chapter 5:

The African Entrepreneurship

Movement

The Importance of Entrepreneurship

One of the reasons why entrepreneurship is so vital to the development of the African economy is its demographic: This is a continent of the young. The average age is far lower than in most

Western developed countries or countries in Asia. The answer to the question of future economic prosperity for Africa must therefore address the ideas, wants, and needs of the youth; it is a key component behind Tony's proposed model of Africapitalism and the unique challenges and opportunities that one comes across there in comparison to the capitalist models which have taken root in other newer economies such as South Korea, China, and India.

Capitalist economies in the West have typically been built on the idea of formal, organized labor which is exchanged for wages, meaning that workers become part of the transaction in seeking profit. However, the majority of the workforce in Africa is actually engaged in informal labor. As a result, today's youthful population of Africa are not content to become just another cog in the larger economic machine, subject to the whims of employers or the chronic instability of the region. Instead, they want to think beyond the informal nature of employment in Africa, and many have decided instead that they do not want to work for anyone else. Studies of these trends in Africa have shown that young people are more interested in starting their own businesses than working in a traditional job, receiving a wage for their labor, or creating wealth for businesses through these means.

It is a change in mindset that Tony has had personal experience of; in 2010, at the same time that he established Heirs Holdings, he set up a major philanthropic venture to drive forward his vision of Africapitalism. The charity, which is known as The Tony Elumelu Foundation (TEF) has made a significant impact in the support of these young Africans who have entrepreneurship on their mind. Through the foundation, Tony has provided seed capital and mentoring to thousands of individuals since its inception.

The importance of supporting entrepreneurship in these ways has been clearly demonstrated by the growth and popularity of the TEF's Entrepreneurship Program. In its nascency, in 2015, the program had around 20,000 applications; by 2022, less than a decade later, applications have grown 20 times over to more than 400,000 (*Africapitalism and Africa's sustainable development*, 2023). This major rise in application numbers demonstrates just how eager young Africans are to start their own companies, rather than going down the more well-trodden career path of seeking success through working hard for someone else and rising through the ranks as white-collar workers to achieve higher and higher wages.

Because of the unpredictability of job markets in Africa over the decades since independence, many young people still find that traditional routes into employment are not open or available to them, even with a strong academic background. Most of the entrepreneurs who have benefitted from Tony's program of support have completed at least a four-year undergraduate degree at university, and yet, they still find that the companies or employment options that await them after graduation are not fit for purpose for their vision and ideas for the future of Africa. This is one of the driving factors behind the popularity of the TEF's program and also illustrates the priorities and interests of the young demographic in general: This generation is not content to follow their parents and grandparents into an unstable, informal job market. This generation wants change.

Additionally, the benefit of supporting such passionate, determined young people in their entrepreneurial journey reaches far beyond the creation of wealth for a few individuals. Investment in entrepreneurial ventures aligns with the change in economic behavior that Africapitalism proposes; it is profit-seeking, not rent-seeking, investment. Many of the TEF program's successes show how this can benefit the social wealth of the wider community, such as by creating jobs in the local area. They also have the effect of inspiring others around them to succeed. Thus, the prosperity of the entrepreneurs themselves has a larger positive impact on Africa; this is ultimately the way to create jobs and drive growth on a continent with such a youthful demographic.

For Tony, it is also about empowering this vital part of the population. He remembers, only too well, the frustrations and obstacles that he himself faced on his journey, both in terms of the financial costs of accessing higher education and the difficulty in securing employment in his chosen field, even with two degrees. He is one of the success stories, but he wants there to be more stories like his in the future.

Tony still lives and works in Lagos, and he is all too aware of the tragedy of youth unemployment that has continued to affect Nigeria and Africa, as a whole. He recognizes the betrayal that young people feel: that they have done everything that the capitalist dream has told them to do—worked hard, studied hard, gained degrees—but still, it is not enough to find a job. He can see the unrest and dissatisfaction that is brewing among them, and he believes that there can only be two outcomes in the near future: a positive use of their ambition, energy, and zeal, or a disastrous one. He wants them to feel part of their nation and be supported to grow and succeed, not in opposition to governments and leaders who they believe are responsible for the lack of opportunities. If the youth feel marginalized, Tony fears, they will bring catastrophe. Entrepreneurship is a surefire way to create employment opportunities that don't currently exist and, moreover, to create a climate in which the youth demographic feel supported and listened to, rather than ignored.

How to Support the Future

Tony's philanthropic program is not the first, nor the only, organization to recognize the importance of young entrepreneurs; over the years, through a mixture of government, NGO, and multinational investment, there has been historical investment in this area. Yet, what makes Tony's support stand out from the crowd is the success that has been achieved by his graduates, whilst many small- and medium-sized enterprises (or SMEs) developed by these other methods have not reaped the same rewards. In order to support Africa's economic development through entrepreneurship, therefore, it is vital that any future investment follows Tony's model.

Firstly, entrepreneurs need access to adequate seed-funding capital in order to actually grow and scale up properly. Financial support has typically been offered to SMEs in the past via loans, not grants, by governments or investors. However, this puts such a significant financial strain on a new business that it can often create too much pressure and discourage creativity and innovation as a result. A grant provides much more flexible, long-term support for entrepreneurs, giving them the freedom to take risks and truly bring their dreams to life. In Africa, access to seed capital has traditionally been limited—

even though this is how the lives of both individuals and communities as a whole are changed.

Even with adequate seed capital, the conditions need to be right for them to flourish: Another major challenge that must be overcome by African entrepreneurs is the overregulation of licenses, high taxes for SMEs, and complex or unnecessary encounters with bureaucratic rules. After independence, many of the new governments or leaders in Africa saw their role as one of control and regulation, which led to an imbalance in some aspects of the public sector. As a result, this has had a negative effect, often inadvertently, on private industry by making it too difficult for businesses to start, operate, or grow within such a climate. Although there has been some improvement in terms of these obstacles over the last two decades, it is still inconsistent across the continent, with some governments leaning into more forward-thinking strategies than others. For entrepreneurship to truly launch the economic development of Africa for the future, more radical tax incentives, exemptions, and breaks for entrepreneurs need to be considered. These would give the private sector the freedom it needs from the way that past regulation and bureaucracy have stifled it.

Investment in entrepreneurship, however, is about much more than the financial aspects. Skills, knowledge, and training are just as crucial in the journey to success. Without an understanding of management, marketing, product development, or accounting, entrepreneurs cannot guide their businesses to make a profit. Individuals won't be able to make informed decisions and scale their ideas from an initial concept into a workable company without the necessary input into their training. Although many entrepreneurs are university graduates, even those with a higher education don't necessarily have the practical, real-life experience of running a business or understanding the world of commerce. Training in how to run a company is crucial to the overall success or failure of a venture. This is something that Tony not only is passionate about but also understands from firsthand experience. He has always been willing to ask for answers and advice from those with knowledge and expertise in certain areas; he always sees his training as ongoing and wants to learn from others wherever he can.

This is why mentorship is so important in supporting future growth. The expertise that already exists in certain industries and regions must be shared with the ambitious young generations of entrepreneurs, whether it is the practical, day-to-day running of a business or an understanding of the limitations of infrastructure and regional connectivity which continue to exist in Africa—two key components that can have a dramatic impact on the potential success and profitability of a fledgling business. If risks and problems can be mitigated in the early stages of the journey through the advice and support of a mentor, a business has a much higher chance of long-term success. Too often, prospective entrepreneurs lack deep knowledge of the market or sector that they wish to join, but mentors can help them to understand where their talents, skills, or ideas best lay within the existing conditions and where they might find the greatest success with their business—without the entrepreneur having to go through the process of trial and error, thus improving their prospect of actually creating a viable business model. The way that the TEF program combines mentoring and financial support is arguably why their success rate is higher than in other instances of investment.

Furthermore, mentorship is not just about practicalities. It is also about keeping the mentee motivated in what can be extremely challenging and stressful circumstances, thus supporting their personal growth as well as their financial one. It is a way to keep young, inexperienced people accountable and on track to achieve their goals, helping them to meet their highest potential. But the best mentoring relationships are collaborative and reciprocal; by partnering with young people who have recently graduated or who have innovative ideas unique to their generation, mentees can also potentially help to stimulate growth or change in the businesses of the mentor as well.

It was with these ideas and concerns always on his mind that Tony, for the last decade, has been working tirelessly to open the eyes of governments and international organizations to the importance of entrepreneurship in Africa and his belief that it holds the key to Africa's future. And it is these beliefs and the typical, Tony Elumelu determination and resilience, that have made Tony accept invitations to events, meetings, and interviews with the media at every opportunity. Since he released his paper on Africapitalism in 2011, he has become an increasingly recognizable personality in Africa and the rest of the world, as a result of this high profile. But this is not about personal gain for Tony: He has been a tireless campaigner for, and champion of, Africa's youth.

This was how he found himself to be the recipient of an invitation to attend the United Nations General Assembly in September 2022. Almost five years after he accepted the Dwight D. Eisenhower Award, Tony was back in New York City on an important mission—this time, in his capacity, not as an individual who was being celebrated for his achievements but as an African leader. He was accustomed to international travel these days: Only the previous week, he had bumped into an old friend, Aliko Dangote—founder of the Dangote Group and one of Africa's richest men—at Lagos airport on his way home from another important trip. Such was the life of a man with a mission to improve the world.

When he stepped off the plane on the 18th of September, 2022, to the backdrop of a glorious sunset from the lingering summer warmth, Tony was struck by the weightiness of what he was in New York to achieve. Far from just being a powerhouse in the world of business, he now had the attention of politicians, campaigners, and researchers. His voice really mattered.

As he traveled into the city for the night from the airport, caught in the usual frenetic traffic of New York, he watched lights begin to flicker on in apartments and townhouses in the residential neighborhoods, then in restaurants, bars, and clubs in the heart of Manhattan—a testament to the old adage that New York never sleeps, even on a Sunday. That evening, thinking of the storm which had raged outside the award ceremony he attended at Cipriani on Wall Street, he watched the throngs of tourists and residents passing by the car windows in their shorts and summer dresses, enjoying the vestiges of an "Indian summer." Used to the sweltering heat of Nigeria, Tony was amused by the way that everyone here seemed determined to soak up every last drop of sunshine and heat, crowding to sit outside at patio tables or in the little neighborhood parks that he passed. Although he had traveled to New York many times during the previous decade, both in his capacity as the chairman of Heirs Holdings and as the founder of the TEF, he never failed to feel energized by the constant thrum of noise and people which permeated its streets or the cultural melting pot of its population.

It was a busy week, with no time to be spent playing tourist in the city on this particular visit. He began, on Monday, by addressing the World Economic Forum (WEF) Friends of Africa Continental Free Trade Area (AfCFTA) as the keynote speaker. Presenting alongside Presidents Adama Barrow, Nana Addo Dankwa Akufo-Addo, and Mokgweetse Eric Masisi—the Presidents of Gambia, Ghana, and Botswana respectively—Tony talked of the importance of intra-African trade and developing US–African trade partnerships, along with spreading his messages of impact, transformation, and Africapitalism on this prestigious international stage.

From there, he was whisked across Manhattan to the headquarters of the United Nations in order to meet with Preeti Sinha, the Executive Secretary of the Capital Development Fund (UNCDF), and to sign an important agreement to support youth entrepreneurship in Africa. Passing the lines of tourists outside the Empire State Building, Tony craned his neck to see its full height and beauty. He wondered if any of the visitors standing at the viewing platform at the top were looking down at his sleek black saloon car as it inched its way forward along the wide avenues of Midtown Manhattan or if they were looking up and across the city's skyline instead.

When the car pulled up outside, the East River glinting in the lunchtime sunlight, he had a moment of surreal disbelief that he was about to set foot into this famous building in a professional capacity. He had the feeling of being a tourist, just like those climbing the heights of the Empire State Building or gliding along the river on an open-topped boat for a tour. A light breeze fluttered the tails of his suit jacket as he approached the grand steps, setting the line of flags off to wave wildly as if beckoning him inside. Tony buttoned his jacket and adjusted his grip on his briefcase, then walked inside to, once again, make history.

Seated beside Preeti at a large wooden table, Tony felt much more at home: It was a space that could have belonged inside any office or conference room in the world, and Tony was certainly no stranger to such meetings. The major difference on this day, however, was the line of reporters and photographers beyond the desk, waiting to snap pictures of them when they raised their pens. The deal between Tony's foundation and the UNCDF had already been agreed upon, so the moment of signing, with them sitting next to each other and opening their matching blue folders containing copies of the extensive document, was more ceremonial than strictly necessary. But Tony recognized its importance. He was being recorded for news bulletins, photographed for newspapers and websites, and live-streamed on social media. It was a moment in which his reach, and thus the reach of his message, was increased beyond his imaginings from when he first sat in his home office in Lagos, trying to find a way to put his beliefs of how to support the future of Africa into writing. Now, he had international backing for his philanthropic venture: This deal was a commitment of resources, technology, and funds to increase Tony's reach across the continent and thus his ability to support even more young entrepreneurs in Africa. He knows that he cannot change the world by himself, and so, partnerships like these are vital if he is to continue to scale up what he is trying to achieve and really make an impact on the future.

In the days that followed the signing, Tony answered questions from numerous reporters, unable to contain his wide smile and buzz of excitement and passion at every meeting, even at the end of a long day. His boundless enthusiasm was broadcast live across America, and beyond, when he appeared on CNN with Richard Quest.

He also attended state dinners with global leaders and dignitaries, shaking hands with some of the most influential people in the world. He met with representatives from Google, the President of Nigeria, the President of the UN General Assembly, and Bill Gates. In every situation, from intimate conversations with individuals to delivering speeches to huge audiences, Tony emanated calm, confidence, and professionalism, his trademark red socks and red tie serving as a reminder, to Tony himself, of the humble man from modest beginnings that he would always be, no matter where or with whom he found himself on this landmark day.

As he shook hands and posed for photographs alongside these dignitaries and politicians, Tony was reminded, with each firm grip or click of a camera, of the privilege that he had managed to achieve as a result of his personal success. He was also reminded, each time a comment or interaction popped up on one of his social media channels, of just how many young, hopeful Africans were looking to him for guidance and inspiration.

"Entrepreneurship," he explained once more, as he concluded his final interview of the week in New York, "is the most effective way to establish true prosperity" (*A conversation with Tony Elumelu...*, 2022). As the journalist nodded and thanked him for his time, Tony hoped that his hard work in securing partnerships with prominent international organizations and speaking so many times on this subject would help the rest of the world believe it too.

The Value of Support

Youth unemployment poses one of the most significant threats to global economic growth. Each year, there are approximately 10 million new young people flooding into the employment market in Africa after graduating from various stages of education. However, it is estimated that there are only ever 3 million new jobs actually available to them. This translates, in practical terms, to three out of every five young Africans being unemployed in some capacity (Ugochukwu, 2021). This is a frightening figure and one that goes to show just how many well-educated university students or graduates there are who are still unable to find employment and embark on a suitable career path.

In fact, today's youth are even more likely than the previous generation to be unemployed. This is partly due to the rapid rise in the demographic, with the labor market and economies of African nations unable to keep up with the demand. But it is also due to the unique circumstances and challenges of the 21st century: The world has lurched from crisis to crisis in the last 20 years, from financial disasters to the COVID-19 pandemic, all of which have had a significant impact on equality. The global lockdowns have decimated the small business sector and created higher unemployment rates in some regions than ever, all whilst the number of billionaires is simultaneously increasing. It is an unsustainable vision of the future.

So, in order to create a stable social and economic situation in Africa, it is vital that the capacity to generate new job opportunities is increased so that this statistic can begin to improve. The potential value of supporting young people in employment is vast, not least because of the impact it would have on Africa's economic growth. When more young people are employed, they can, of course, contribute to productivity and lead to an increase in GDP through a developmental dividend. But this value is much more multifaceted and broad than this: As youth unemployment is so closely linked with continuing poverty, increased employment can also help to reduce poverty levels across the continent as they increase their incomes and improve their living standards. This is because, when viable avenues of job and wealth creation are established, these employment options can provide young people with their chance to lift themselves out of the cycle of hardship that has been perpetuated for too many generations in Africa. When they acquire more experience in their career, they acquire new skills and knowledge, much of which can similarly be applied in other areas of their lives, such as personal finance or political engagement. It creates well-rounded citizens who, in turn, contribute to the quality of the workforce and are more engaged in their local and national communities and civic activities. This not only helps to build a more competitive economy through the upskilling of labor but also creates a more democratic, participatory society, where social instability and political unrest are less likely to occur.

According to the United Nations Population Fund, if countries in sub-Saharan Africa are able to make the right investments to support young people, they could find that the added value amounts to as much as $500 billion a year—about a third of the region's current GDP—for as many as 30 years. Similarly, the World Economic Forum, estimates that Nigeria's GDP could be around 29% higher by 2030 if the right policies and investments in human and social capital are made (*The power of 1.8 Billion...*, 2014).

It's clear to see that the potential is huge for the next decade. If the youth population are provided with the right skills, training, and opportunities when they come of age, their creativity, innovation, and entrepreneurial spirit could have the biggest impact on economic growth and development that the continent has ever seen.

The vast majority of firms—which are therefore responsible for generating most of the jobs—across Africa are micro, small, and medium businesses. Youth entrepreneurs make up an important sector of these enterprises, and they are more likely to employ their peers and be active in high-growth areas (*Youth entrepreneurship and innovation…*, n.d.). If properly supported, they could be the key to opening up the job market and creating some of the millions of new opportunities needed to try and reduce unemployment.

Tony is one of the strongest advocates of supporting young people in this way. He knows that investing in their training and ideas will be critical to unlocking the continent's potential, but he also understands that this is not just a one-way process, with young people being the passive recipients of financial or educational support. They have fresh, innovative ideas about how to solve some of the problems that have been plaguing their nations for years, especially in regard to climate emergency, sustainable development, and the use of emerging technologies. He also understands that being an entrepreneur doesn't necessarily mean running your own business—even in terms of a microenterprise. It is also about having an entrepreneurial mindset, no matter where you work or what your job is.

Thinking like an entrepreneur, just as Tony has always done, means carving out or creating your own opportunities, growing in whatever role you find yourself in, and seeing the world differently. Young people already see the world differently in so many ways and have different concerns and ambitions from previous generations. They are, therefore, perfectly placed to redefine what business and the job market will look like in the future of Africa. They need the support of established leaders and research in order to reach their potential, but ultimately it will be the youth themselves who will bring new products, methods of production, and competition to the world of commerce. This is why, as part of his investment group, Heirs Holdings, Tony set up his foundation; in many ways, he sees the training and support of young people as just as valuable, and potentially just as profitable, as the companies such as Transcorp which he acquired.

Chapter 6:

The Tony Elumelu Foundation

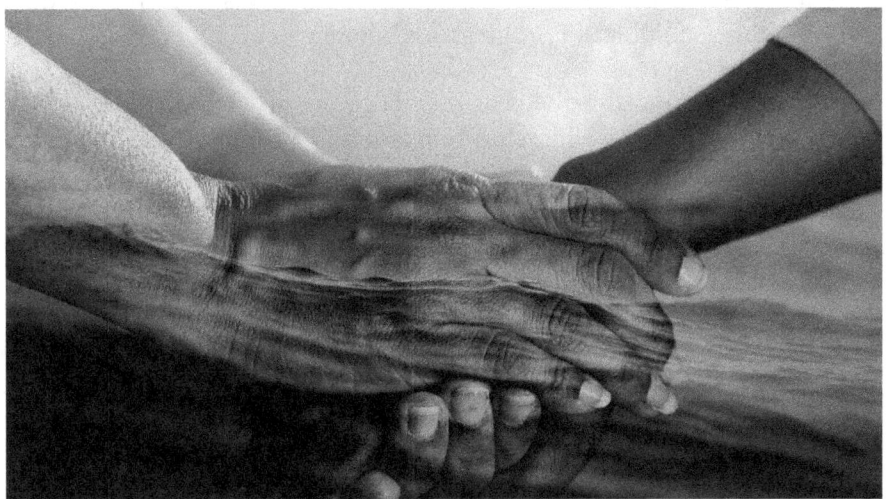

The Start of TEF

The year 2010 was a time of significant change, both economically and socially, in Africa. After the American economic crash in 2008, which influenced a global economic downturn in the years that followed, 2010 was a time in which many African countries began to experience growth. Driven by improved policies, increased investment, and the rising prices of commodities, it was a year that demonstrated the potential and opportunity that Africa represented, even while many challenges and obstacles continue to exist. The continent actually had the fastest average rate of GDP growth of any region between 2005 and 2010—real GDP grew by an average of 4.7% (*Trade growth to ease...*, 2010).

In Nigeria, the success of Goodluck Jonathan in the presidential election in May 2010 created an important period of relative stability and demonstrated the nation's support for democracy, following decades of swinging back and forth to military rule. This led to a change in legislation and some macroeconomic policies that stimulated even more GDP growth than in other parts of Africa—expanding by 8.4% in 2010 as a result of high oil prices and the improvement of conditions in which businesses could operate. It was, therefore, a time of economic and political progress for Nigeria.

The year 2010 was also the year that Tony set up Heirs Holdings and, alongside it, the Tony Elumelu Foundation (TEF). It was an ideal time to set up both a major investment group—in order to capitalize on the major expansion in GDP—and a philanthropic organization because the rapid growth that was being experienced was still characterized by huge inequality. Despite the rise in average GDP, unemployment and poverty remained very high, particularly among young people, and the Foundation was launched as a way to try to redress this balance through sharing funds and education with entrepreneurs.

The need for equality has always been personal to Tony. He has never lost sight of the role that luck has played in his own life and career, no matter how much wealth and influence he has accumulated. In essence, the more he has succeeded on a personal level, the more he has felt the pull to give something back to Africa. When he decided to leave UBA Group for the next stage of his career, he was considering the ways in which he could spread luck, hope, and opportunities just as much as how he could pursue other business opportunities. To Tony, the Foundation was a way to leverage the power, wealth, and privilege he had achieved to benefit the next generation of African entrepreneurs.

On his last day as UBA Group chairman, Tony waited for the elevator, one more time, to transport him down to ground level. It was something he had done every day, for years, and he felt a wave of emotion as he stood beside coworkers sharing final messages of farewell and best wishes. But it was not sadness that he felt; it was excitement, and hope. He was ready for a new challenge after conquering the world of finance so successfully.

The last person to shake his hand that day was one of the bank's youngest employees, who dashed to catch up to him as he crossed the lobby to the street entrance. There was gratitude in the young man's eyes, and respect in his voice, as he wished Tony luck in his next endeavors. It was a message that Tony considered carefully on the car journey home—a reminder that, without luck and mentorship in his early career, he would not be where he was on that day. He wondered where he would have been instead without encountering the people who gave him a chance as a young, inexperienced graduate.

The plan for a philanthropic venture had already been in the pipeline for a number of months, but when Tony arrived home that night, he made a vow: that he would institutionalize luck and democratize access to the kind of success and opportunities that he himself had had the good fortune to encounter. Paying this forward would become his lifelong mission.

However, after the Foundation's launch in 2010, Tony quickly discovered that his personal mission and commitment were going to be tested by the world in which he was operating. Nigeria lacked appropriate legislation to regulate charities, as well as the means to hold these organizations to account.

Yet, Tony did not let the lack of strategic legislation hold him, or the TEF, back. Instead, he took matters into his own hands; just as he had done by drafting his political and ideological vision for economic development, Tony put pen to paper once more. He wrote the nation's first Charity Act, outlining the ways in which a stronger, more transparent, and impactful social sector should be built. The draft legislation called for the certification of all nonprofit organizations, tax incentives for donor corporations and individuals, and appropriate penalties and appeals processes where necessary. It was intended to ensure that all philanthropic institutions, including TEF, operated efficiently and achieved their stipulated goals. He presented it to the Attorney General of the Federation.

Although it has yet to be codified into legal practice, and reform is still desperately needed in the sector, the influence of this kind of lobbying has been clear to see in other ways, not least in the recent changes to tax law to reduce inequality and support small businesses since 2020.

The more that Tony has worked alongside the government in all his guises, from financial advice to social champion, the more they have taken note of his expertise.

Since 2010, he has worked hard on the Foundation, alongside his duties at Heirs Holdings, trying to reach as many young entrepreneurs as possible across Africa and set up new opportunities wherever possible. His commitment has helped him to reach far and wide.

In 2012, he partnered with former British Prime Minister Tony Blair to set up the Blair–Elumelu Fellowship Program, supporting government agencies in Liberia and Sierra Leone to set up the Public Private Partnership Unit and National Investment Commission, helping to promote Africapitalism in two of the most poverty-stricken countries in the region. The same year, as part of an initiative involving social technology, he provided seed funding for 20 innovative ventures, supporting the experimentation and development of prototypes to accelerate the adoption of new technology.

In 2012, he also set up The Nigeria Fast Growth 50, or Nigeria50, a body representing the fastest and most dynamic unlisted private companies—exactly the type of businesses that he hoped to support long-term because they had the biggest potential for entrepreneurship and were responsible for the highest numbers of job creation. He helped the companies gain global visibility and new sources of investment, as well as supporting some individuals who he saw as emerging stars in the workforce.

Then, there was the Elumelu Professionals Program—an MBA internship for some of the bright new minds in African business. It focused on leadership potential, placing students from top business schools, across both African and Western universities, in internship programs at successful companies in order to build the students' real-world business experience. From forging strategies to marketing new products, Tony brought African and international students together, opening up the potential of African businesses and markets to the next generation of successful leaders.

He also set up the Tony and Awele Elumelu Prize to recognize academic excellence. Between 2012 and 2015, they gave 130 students in

Nigerian and West African Universities prize money to support them in their studies, help break down barriers caused by inequality, and encourage more students from disadvantaged backgrounds to attend undergraduate or postgraduate education.

As applications to the charity and its programs increased year after year, Tony sought partnerships and further funding commitments from other organizations in order to expand their capacity. The United Nations Development Program, the African Development Bank, the International Committee of the Red Cross, and the German development agency, *Gesellschaft für Internationale Zusammenarbeit* (GIZ)—Tony approached them all, bringing the might and influence of these institutions on board in the effort to create meaningful, long-term change.

He supported the creation of the Impact Economy Innovations Fund—a joint initiative with the Rockefeller Foundation, providing funding for mobile technology, finance, advocacy, and agriculture across Africa.

But as demand for each of these awards, schemes, and programs continued to soar, and Tony came across more and more high-quality applications and talented individuals, he began to wonder if he would ever be able to do enough to really support the thousands of young people who were so clearly relying on him for his help. So, Tony redoubled his efforts, seeking to expand the foundation on an even larger scale and find a solution to this question.

Tony's Mission

Five years after its initial inception, Tony launched the TEF's flagship program: the Tony Elumelu Foundation Entrepreneurship Program (TEEP). In 2015, he announced that this program would, over the next 10 years, become a $100 million initiative that was aimed at supporting 10,000 young African entrepreneurs with training, mentorship, and the seed capital needed to start and grow their businesses. With this new commitment, the Foundation—and Tony himself—became the leading champion of entrepreneurship in Africa. By rerouting funding and resources into a single, streamlined effort, he was able to focus fully on entrepreneurship and help to create businesses that have the most potential when it comes to creating jobs, generating revenue, and contributing to their local communities.

Now active across all 54 African countries, the TEEP program was designed to build on the Foundation's initial success and empower more young people, identifying and supporting a new generation of the most promising entrepreneurs across Africa. It offered another avenue through which Tony could implement his mission to share the philosophy of Africapitalism and empower young people. From the TEEP program and advocacy to research and the annual TEF Forum—the largest gathering of entrepreneurs in Africa—Tony has poured all of his business expertise and leveraged all of the strength of his reputation into building a philanthropic organization that has a real impact on the lives of communities.

The holistic program of the TEEP offers effective, intensive support to the entrepreneurs that it supports. It starts with a 12-week program that teaches the basic skills of development, marketing, management, and product design needed to launch a business. After this initial stage, program participants are provided with online mentoring from world-class business leaders who are carefully matched to their needs and challenges. They also gain access to a bespoke online library that expounds upon both the skills they learned in the first learning period, as well as Tony's own business values and the philosophy of Africapitalism. They learn how to develop a clear business plan, scale up, add value to their local community, and have a meaningful impact on social wealth. Tony aims, by sharing his ideology as well as the more practical aspects of running a business, to mold them into models in his own image and ensure the spread of ideas which is vital to the widespread success of the public and private cooperation that he envisages.

But the program is not just about mentoring and education. Each venture receives $5,000 of seed capital to support its growth and enhance its ideas. For many, this money is the lifeblood they need to get their business off the ground: without it, their innovative and creative ideas would remain just that—ideas, not viable business opportunities.

At key dates in the year, the Foundation hosts meet-ups across nations and states to promote strong professional relationships and encourage networking between the entrepreneurs taking part in the program, as well as offer them the opportunity to discuss challenges and roadblocks with local agencies or government officials. There is also a huge forum each year, bringing everyone together, to demonstrate the potential power and influence that the program holds. The recipients of the program also have the ability to keep in touch with others through the alumni network, which matches graduates of the training course according to the sector and location in which they are operating. This aims to foster the kind of relationships that Tony knows are vital for success in the business world, as well as a healthy sense of competition which is an important part of the capitalist model.

So far, the Foundation has trained over 1.5 million Africans and dispersed millions of dollars in direct funding to 18,000 African men and women. They have collectively created over 400,000 direct and indirect jobs—a significant contribution to the much-needed social wealth and development, as well as GDP growth, on the continent (*Africapitalism and Africa's sustainable development*, 2023).

As the entrepreneurship program has continued to grow, Tony's mission and direction have also begun to evolve. Although he continues to focus on private-sector-led growth as the means to foster economic development, particularly through the sponsorship of entrepreneurship, he is increasingly focused on promoting sustainable development.

The world is becoming more aware of the impending climate emergency, but no one is more aware of its consequences than the people of Africa. They experience, every day, the natural disasters which are caused by climate change, and they are the victims who are most affected by its impact—even though they are not responsible for the pollution and carbon consumption that has caused it. When he began to witness too many missed opportunities by those in the West to create meaningful change, Tony made an important decision: to ensure that sustainability was moved to the core of everything that Heirs Holdings and the Foundation did.

Tony has always been at the forefront of innovation in business, and this is no different. His mission now encompasses the imperative to engage with international issues and policy on the subject and to apply strategies that ensure the reduction of impact on the natural environment and resources. Within Heirs Holdings, which has a significant stake in the oil and natural gas industry, he has been working to develop the methods of production and delivery necessary to create a sustainable energy network in Nigeria and beyond. Through the Foundation, similarly, he has championed the efforts of the United Nations' Sustainable Development Goals (SDG) across Africa. The SDG's goals are closely aligned with Tony's, particularly in the way it's working towards the eradication of poverty, the promotion of quality education and gender equality, and the development of industry, innovation, and infrastructure which is especially focused on new sectors and technologies, such as those working towards solutions to the climate emergency. In 2018, he also joined the board of the UN Global Compact, an ambitious corporate sustainability initiative that encourages businesses around the world to implement responsible practices and protect the environment as they operate. The board is made up of CEOs and influential leaders, like Tony, who have volunteered to work towards achieving a better world and who see the importance of businesses taking shared responsibility for the future.

In conjunction with the training courses and online mentoring which are so integral to the young entrepreneurs' success, Tony also considered how best to leverage new technologies as part of their flagship program. This led to the launch of TEFConnect, the largest digital platform to support African entrepreneurs in the world. As a fully online ecosystem, TEFConnect provides a central hub for entrepreneurs, investors, and business leaders in Africa, bringing them together in a mutually beneficial platform. Like the alumni network, annual forum, and other networking events, it allows participants in the program and the wider business community to connect and form the strong relationships which are crucial to the success of Africapitalism. In addition, it provides access to Tony's business toolkit, which includes financial planning calculators, business plan generators, and marketing templates. By adding the online platform to the existing framework in 2018, and building on their initial successes, the Foundation was able to widen the reach of Tony's philanthropic work. There are now 1.5 million registered users on TEFConnect, demonstrating how Tony has been able to democratize access to opportunity and scale up their impact across many more regions and individuals.

Just like Africapitalism, the Foundation's mission is to empower entrepreneurs, enable each new launch and improvement to the program, and therefore aid the journeys of the participants, helping to unleash their potential.

Success Stories

The program is well on its way to achieving the goal, that Tony set in 2015, of helping 10,000 entrepreneurs over the next 10 years. All across the continent, the impact of the Foundation is being felt.

In 2022, they received a total of 381,887 applications from interests ranging from agriculture to fashion to ICT. The majority of these businesses were still in their idea stage or infancy, thus seeking the depth of education, support, and philosophy provided by the TEEP. Of the hundreds of thousands of applications, 1,460 were selected as beneficiaries of some, or all, of Tony's philanthropic support (*Tips for young professionals*, 2022). Over previous years, the most prominent and successful graduates from the program have covered a similar range of industries and ideas.

One such success story is Msindazwe Ndhlovu, who started The Noble Savage Ltd with Tony's seed capital. The company recycles waste plastic to manufacture durable, lightweight, and strong building materials, such as roof tiles and paving blocks. It is a project which not only aligns with the mission of sustainable development and environmentally friendly resources but also proposes to help solve the housing shortage in Africa—one plastic tile and block at a time. Thanks to the Foundation's intervention, Ndhlovu has increased his workforce from five to eight workers, creating more employment opportunities for his peers, and doubled his yearly turnover. He is now in dialogue with an international firm to raise more capital and further scale his award-winning green business.

Chioma Ogbydimkpa is similarly working in the sustainability sector. Her venture, Redbutton, creates professional clothes for women, fusing traditional African prints with innovative eco-friendly materials. The brand promotes African stories and powerful women through the vibrant colors, textures, and designs. Now, her clothes are sold globally online, as well as in local and international retail outlets. The company is her passion—she learned her trade from her mom, who also worked in fashion—but being a green champion is equally important to her. This led her to experiment with innovative materials made from agri-waste—including water hyacinths and coconut shells—and recycled fabrics, creating her statement pieces through sustainable means. Like The Noble Savage Ltd, her company now has more employees, generates a significantly higher income, and has won awards—largely as a result of her selection for the Foundation.

There are also many TEF alumni in the tech space. These include Nicholas Alifa, whose startup has created a range of smart solutions for farmers, bridging the gaps in the food and agricultural chains. Based in Nigeria, Ajaoko Agritech Ltd has built a network that allows farmers to sell directly to consumers through efficient online marketing and distribution platforms. Thanks to the introduction of this new technology, there has been a significant impact on the production and distribution of food. But the platforms are also designed to be quick and easy to use, communicating using simple language that can be understood by all their partners, including rural farmers who have limited access to education.

Nicholas also supports further improvements in the sector through his Agribusiness Academy, which offers high-quality online and onsite training courses to farmers to help improve their processing and management of their businesses—an entrepreneurial idea that helps to maximize the output of the farmers and combat issues of food security, while also creating more products and partnerships for Ajaoka Agritech at the same time. His approaches towards improving this vital sector in Africa, whilst also making a profit for his business, are the perfect example of Africapitalism in action.

But Nicholas's journey has been far from easy or straightforward. Because of the important nature of his ideas, he had already been granted seed capital to launch the business before he entered the TEF Program. However, without the training or business acumen to use the capital most effectively, the grant did not help him achieve the success that he was hoping for. This is where Tony's promotion of knowledge and expertise is what ultimately saved the business: He needed training just as much as he needed a financial contribution. In this way, he was given a second chance through the Foundation.

The training similarly proved crucial to Angele Messa. She received $5,000 of seed capital from the Foundation to build her online learning platform, EduClick Africa, which promotes access to education and facilitates employment access for young people through her jobs search engine, the largest in Cameroon. But it was the business management education that she received through Tony's program that she really credits with her success, rather than the finance. It gave her the tools to be able to develop a business plan, set realistic goals, and work towards achieving them.

While some of the Foundation's success stories have already begun to make real, long-term impacts on African industry and society, others have ideas or products which take longer to bring to market but nonetheless have huge potential. For example, Mohamed Dhaouafi is developing affordable 3D-printed bionic arms for amputees. This has been a problem in Africa for many decades, as too many Africans can't afford prosthetics. But his development of innovative 3D-printed hands and arms has allowed marginalized members of society to function in the world and live their lives to the fullest. One of the main challenges in the development of the business has been the focus on affordability, but that remains at the heart of Mohamed's model: For him, equal access to opportunity and improving quality of life are key. Despite the challenges he has faced, he has been designing and testing bionic arms with resilience and determination and is now ready to begin trials and bring this life-changing technology to the open market.

There are thousands more individuals who have benefited from Tony's philanthropic work. Some have achieved national or global recognition for their ideas; others have operated on a smaller scale, creating one or two extra jobs in their local area or providing a service or product somewhere it previously didn't exist. But no matter the extent or size of their venture, they all have one important thing in common on their journey: the good fortune to have received funding and advice from Tony Elumelu. It is one of the things that makes Tony so unique—his continuing belief that "if the wealth we have is not inclusive, if the prosperity we have is just for family and self, it will not help us create the society we need" (*UBA founder, Tony Elumelu, urges...*, 2019).

Chapter 7:

Global Impact

Tony at 60

On March 22nd, 2023, Tony celebrated his 60th birthday in Lagos. There was a lavish party held at the amphitheater at UBA House—a special symposium that continued late into the night with live music and numerous toasts to the guest of honor. Beginning with presentations and messages of thanks from a host of alumni from the Foundation, it was a testament to his impact that the room was full of gratitude. Attended by his family, friends, colleagues, and some of Nigeria's most prominent celebrities, it was certainly an event to remember.

Many of the guests who were there called it the highlight of the year's social calendar. These included Jim Ovia, one of Tony's fellow "cowboys," the founder of Zenith Bank, and a prominent philanthropist in his own right, who often collaborates with Tony on charitable initiatives; Kennedy Uzoka, the Group Managing Director of UBA, who has worked alongside Tony for many decades in various capacities within the bank; and Parminder Vir OBE, the former CEO of the Foundation and a close friend. Also in attendance were Samuel Nwanze and Emmanuel Nnorom of Heirs Holdings; Oscar N. Onyema, former CEO of the Nigerian Stock Exchange; and Owen Omogiafo, President and Group CEO of Transcorp, one of Heirs Holdings' key investments.

For a man whose birth, six decades earlier in a small town in Plateau State, had been so humble, it is astonishing to consider just how far he has come. Tony's family has been a constant source of inspiration and support, providing him with the love and encouragement he needed to pursue his dreams and make a difference in the world. He has always believed that family is the foundation of everything he does, including his parents and siblings, with whom he is still very close, as well as his wife and children. He is grateful for the role that family has played in shaping his life and career and the way that Dr Awele has supported him in his mission, working alongside him closely on the board of the Foundation to promote their shared values with the world.

Throughout the day, Tony was inundated with birthday messages from world leaders and former presidents and prime ministers, including Bill Clinton and Tony Blair. The outpouring of goodwill was a clear indication of the high esteem in which he is held by the international community, as well as the global impact that he has had over the course of his financial, philanthropic, and business careers.

As of today, he is one of the leading investors and entrepreneurs in Africa and one of the most innovative leaders of a generation. It is no wonder, therefore, that he has been recognized in recent years with a host of prestigious awards and titles, including the Dwight D. Eisenhower Global Entrepreneurship Award, where we began our story. In many cases, he has been the first African to win these prizes, emphasizing just how many boundaries he has transcended, and just much he has done to bring hope to the population of Africa. From

Banker of the Year (African Banker Magazine in 2008) and African Leader of the Year (Investor Magazine in 2016) to one of Africa's 20 Most Powerful in 2012 (Forbes) and Commander of the Order of Federal Republic of Nigeria in 2022, Tony has been celebrated for both his career and his service.

Tony was also named as one of the 100 Most Influential People of 2020 by TIME Magazine, an accolade that puts him among some of the best-known leaders on the planet this century. It is an indication, to the world, that you are someone worth taking note of and remembering. As TIME Magazine explains: "The people on the list, each in their own way, have lessons to teach... down to the last person, they have the power to make us think. And they are using it" (Gibbs, 2016).

Tony is certainly someone who has used his power and influence in this way. He is a billionaire, worth nearly 2 billion U.S. dollars, and yet he uses each moment in the limelight—whether he is accepting awards, giving media interviews, or attending important political events—to further his ideological standpoint and societal impact, not his commercial interests. Time and again, when you hear Tony speak, it is about the changes he hopes to bring to the future, the need for the private sector to support Africa, and the entrepreneurs whose lives he has already changed for the better. With every mention of this tenacious commitment to the charitable sector and political research, he empowers the men and women that he has spent the last decade championing. It is, perhaps, unsurprising that there have been an increasing number of calls, especially on social media, for Tony to present himself as a candidate for the presidency in Nigeria.

Outside of business and family, Tony has also pursued a range of personal interests and passions. He is an avid reader and a lover of art and culture, and he has always been interested in exploring new ideas and learning about new cultures and experiences. One of Tony's most meaningful personal projects has been the Elumelu Art Collection, which is a collection of African and African-inspired art that he has curated over the years. The collection is designed to celebrate the diversity and creativity of African art and culture and to provide a platform for African artists to showcase their work on a global stage.

Through Tony's family, personal interests, and philanthropic duty, he has learned the importance of balance and perspective in life. Over the course of his 60 years, he has come to appreciate that success is not just about achieving professional goals but also finding meaning and purpose in all aspects of life and making a positive impact in the world.

Looking to the Future

The previous March, just after his 59th birthday, Tony was invited to Dubai to accept another prize: the TIME100 Impact Award. During his acceptance speech, he renewed his call to action to the leaders and celebrities who were in attendance. "The world is in need of people like us—more than ever before," he told them (Popli, 2022). There was an urgency to his speech that reflects the many crises the world is currently facing, from the environmental to the humanitarian.

It is also a reflection of the fact that Tony believes African people, businesses, and interests must not be left behind in the future. Although its citizens experience the impact of these crises on a daily basis—particularly those related to climate change, despite the fact that the continent as a whole makes only a minuscule contribution to global emissions—their voices have not always been heard in the conversations around the solutions to these problems. Tony, however, believes that Africa shouldn't just be part of the conversation; he wants to set the agenda for those talks and play an active role in the direction that they take.

For Tony, the impending threat is very real and present. He is a dedicated husband and father, and he feels an increasing sense of responsibility to change the future in which his children will grow up.

When African governments have so many priorities that are already adding competing demands on the time and funding available—from poverty to education to healthcare—they need strong leaders like Tony to be their representatives on the global stage. Through his partnerships with various branches of the United Nations and his close relationships with politicians and businessmen alike, including Jim Ovia with whom he first set out on this trajectory, Tony brings attention to the scale of the task that exists on the ground in Africa to solve the crises that the world is facing. The world cannot afford to ignore, or forget, Africa in its strategies.

Ahead of the COP27 in September 2022, Tony could be found engaging in intense talks with key figures on this subject, including U.S. Senator John Kerry. In a nondescript hotel room—the kind that Tony is all too used to calling home, as he continues his advocacy for Africa around the world—he relished the chance to explain Africa's potential, and the need for collective action, to the Senator in his charming yet relentless style.

Through these meetings and his interviews with TV and print journalists around the world, Tony's mission is about more than just sharing facts with relevant stakeholders: It is just as much about winning hearts and minds and changing the narrative which has surrounded Africa for too long. He wants the world to leave behind the belief that charitable aid is the only way to help the continent rise out of poverty and the challenges it continues to face. Instead, he wants the world to see what young Africans are truly like.

He wants the world to see that the youth of Africa are brave and resilient—that they have already overcome more challenges than most, right from birth, and yet still have ambition. They are more ambitious, and tireless, in their fight for rights and financial security than previous generations. They may be disillusioned and isolated because the political systems, governments, and historical inequalities have let them down so many times in their lives, but they remain vital to change, even when they have already experienced such hardship, because they increasingly have the power to change the future. There are millions of young people in Africa, thanks to the effect of the population bulge which has occurred, and so, there is a power in the collective influence that they could bring to bear.

Collective action can influence reform. This is why Tony has also been focusing on ways that he can connect straight to the youth population. It's not just with politicians and world leaders that he wants to open up a dialogue with about the future of the continent but also with aspiring entrepreneurs, especially those feeling disconnected from their nation, who could actually have the most direct impact on the future of Africa. This is one of the reasons why the Foundation set up TEFConnect, their huge online platform, to stimulate conversations and interactions between the young and the experienced, like Tony himself. But Tony has gone further to reach out on a personal level. He has even written a letter of personal encouragement, addressed *Dear Young African*, published on the Foundation's website, for those who might be in need of direction or mentorship. The letter is as much about politics and holding leaders to account as it is about business, proving the extent of Tony's passion to influence the future and enact real social change. He cares deeply about the journeys that young people will make in their lives and about using the wealth, influence, and experience that he has accrued to support others wherever he can.

Tony also uses social media effectively to engage with this target audience and to interact with those who benefit from his work. He regularly posts inspiring images on Instagram, from both his professional and personal life, and has amassed over a million followers and his own hashtag, *TOEWay*, which has gathered thousands of posts. As he has always avoided too much focus on his family during media interviews and work-related events, his social media profiles are a heartwarming insight into a busy life with his seven children. This is not a family of celebrities but real and relatable people, enjoying social events, from weddings and holiday dinners to fundraising, together. There are some posed photos, of course, but also many candid ones of genuine smiles and goofy dance moves that remind us that Tony is still just the charming, determined boy from Jos, working in the light of his kerosene lamp—and the teenager dreaming of wearing suspenders and brogues to work in a big city bank every day—despite all of his success. This, in itself, is part of the inspirational aura which exudes from the page: that this is what an ordinary man, from a humble background, has managed to achieve. It serves, similarly, as a reminder of the importance of family and the way that he has always made a point of prioritizing his time with them and creating meaningful connections, despite his incredibly busy professional life, with both his work and philanthropic efforts taking him on so many journeys around the world.

Social media does not just provide an insight into Tony's personal life, however, or a way to reach a wider audience of future entrepreneurs.

He also uses it, in the present moment, to form a bridge between the workers or business leaders of Nigeria and the officials and agencies that he is able to talk to directly. He is, in this way, an advocate for the conditions and challenges that people are affected by in their own practical experiences of running operations in different sectors, and he's always willing to listen to the stories and suggestions of others, just as he has been from the start of his career. On one memorable occasion, ahead of a meeting with the government in Nigeria on tax law and tax processes, he put out a call on Twitter for people to share the obstacles they faced as a result of the existing tax systems. There was, as you can imagine, a huge response, and Tony actively listened to what they had to say. He used their messages and tweets as the basis for his talk with the officials, becoming the conduit through which their voices could be heard in official settings. Afterward, it was clear that these issues had actually been heard; there was a shift in policy announced, and Tony was clearly an influential figure in the process (Dizolele, 2022). He has similarly conducted question-and-answer sessions on Facebook and live streams, speaking with and replying to people from all parts of Africa and walks of life, cementing his popularity and revered status across the continent.

Playing the role of the mediator in this way is a vital part of Tony's continuing relevance on the global stage and the urgency for change that he is trying to impart to stakeholders and international leaders. He is, as his inclusion on the TIME100 list can attest to, hugely influential and someone that is listened to around the world. This is why he makes the most of the opportunities he is given to speak up, often on behalf of those who have been marginalized or ignored for decades in the past.

There is a growing sense that Africa is standing on the precipice of huge change at the moment. There is more support for mobilizing and creating collective action and challenging the existing leadership structures. But this is a turning point: Change needs to happen soon in order to capitalize on the advantages of population growth, emerging markets, and investment opportunities that currently exist. Speaking at the Africa Now Conference in Kampala in 2019, Tony delivered his verdict about the race to secure this future: "We need leaders who understand and care about creating a positive legacy. We need leaders who are genuinely committed and care about the future of Africa…

We need to take collective responsibility for our own future" (*UBA founder, Tony Elumelu, urges…*, 2019).

Since he began his work on Africapitalism, he has seen significant progress in Africa, from the emergence of new industries and markets to the growing influence of African leaders and entrepreneurs, like himself, on the global stage. But there is still much work to be done, and he believes that the future of African business will be defined by innovation, collaboration, and a deep commitment to creating positive change.

Epilogue:

Lessons & Reflections

As I come to the end of Tony's biography, I am grateful for the opportunity to reflect on such a life and career and to share Anthony O. Elumelu's story with you. I am filled with a sense of gratitude and purpose. I am grateful for the opportunities and experiences that have shaped this unique man's life and for the people who have been part of this epic tale of business, philanthropy, and service. And I am filled with a sense of purpose as a result of the inspiration he offers, knowing that there is still much work to be done but that Tony is still playing an active role in shaping the future.

Through the ups and downs, the successes and failures, the joys and challenges, he has learned that life is a journey and that success is not just about achieving goals but also finding meaning and purpose in all aspects of life. He has been guided by a deep commitment to making a positive difference in the world, promoting social responsibility and sustainable growth, and supporting the development of African business and entrepreneurship. And he remains committed to these values at the age of 60, knowing that they are more important now for Africa than ever before. He's excited to continue on his journey even further, working with others to create a brighter future for all. Whether through business, entrepreneurship, philanthropy, or public service, he knows that there is much that can be achieved when we work together and that the possibilities are endless.

As we reflect on his life and career, there are many lessons that we can learn from his experiences and perspective on the world. Here's my take on how to live your life the *TOE Way*:

- **Work hard:** Tony's meteoric rise to success—from his humble beginnings in Jos to his role as an influential leader—is a testament to the power of hard work and determination. At every junction in his journey and at every potential stumbling block, Tony redoubled his efforts, focused his mind, and worked until he had achieved his goal. He has always believed that success is not just about talent or intelligence but also the willingness to work hard, persevere, and never give up. Resilience and strength can be the key to unlocking potential, even when challenges or obstacles seem to be stacked against you—just look at Tony. Put in the hours of research, the late nights, the diligence, the extra job applications, or the drive for promotions and pay raises, and you will be rewarded in the end.

- **Set goals:** Goals provide a roadmap to your success. Whether small or highly ambitious, goals ensure that you know where you're heading and where to concentrate your time, energy, and effort. They help you to be disciplined and resilient but also to ensure that the hard work you put in is focused in the right area. Goals also help you look ahead, ensuring that, at each milestone, you are thinking of the bigger picture and the end destination of your journey. It is what motivated Tony, at each stage of his career, to keep moving forward and ensure that his plans and strategies, such as for the success of his banks, were always aspirational.

- **Reflect:** When you reach a goal or your first milestone toward success, it means that you know where you are heading. But it is also important to look back at what you have learned along the way. Reflect on the path you have taken and the energy that you have expended. Think about how you have measured success and what you can do to recalibrate or improve the journey. Tony has always followed this practice, regularly asking himself if his goals continued to be aligned with long-term aims or if something needed to change along the way; flexibility and the willingness to evaluate your progress are key to sustainable success. Yet, it is important not to lose sight, as you adapt and improve, of what you have already achieved; celebrate each win, no matter how small it may seem in the grand scheme of things.

- **Work together:** No one can achieve success alone, and Tony has been fortunate to have the support and encouragement of many people throughout his life and career, from his parents and family to his managers and mentors in his early career. Tony has been the recipient of luck and good fortune, but he has also understood the power of relationships and collaboration from the start, and this has helped him to rise to the top. To Tony, we are all connected, and we can achieve greatness when we work together. What's more, we can really bring about change and reform through community and collective action—the future is ours for the taking.

- **Believe in yourself:** Tony's career in banking may have started with luck, but it was the belief that he was good enough for the role, despite what the paperwork seemed to suggest, that made him put an application forward, and that was ultimately what led him to receive his initial banking position just as much as the chairman's diligent reading of each letter. Whatever your dreams and however far they might seem to be out of reach, they are valid. It's good to want more; let your desires and aspirations fuel your energy to achieve the results you want.

- **Give back:** It is Tony's mission to give back to the world and try to offer others the same luck and support that he has received in his own life. Personal wealth is not his goal; he wants success and opportunity to be shared and to create an equitable society where everyone can enjoy a better world. He has been a fierce champion for creating social wealth, using his resources and platform as an influential speaker to make a positive impact on the world. Whether through philanthropy, public service, or entrepreneurship, he has always sought to make a meaningful difference in the lives of others. We all have a collective responsibility to use our talents and resources to create positive change in whatever capacity we can offer. As you climb the ladder to success, turn back to those behind you, and train or inspire them to follow in your footsteps as well.

- **Remember your balance**: If you are single-minded in your approach, it can be easy to forget the importance of other parts of your life. Success is not just defined in terms of wealth or a thriving career. Relationships, family, good health, a sense of purpose—these things can be just as rewarding, albeit in different ways, and the secret to true success is finding the right time to work hard and move forward, according to what is most important to you at the time.

I hope that this biography will serve as a source of inspiration and encouragement to others, as Tony's life has to me, and that it will help to promote the values of hard work, determination, community, collaboration, and social responsibility that have guided Tony's life and career.

Thank you, reader, for joining me on this journey. And, finally, thank you to Tony O. Elumelu, and everything that he has already given back to the world, for leading us all by his example.

About the Author

Ope Adeleke is an accomplished author, an experienced healthcare professional, and a talented motivational coach. With over two decades of experience in mental health and rehabilitation, Ope has dedicated his career to helping individuals overcome personal and emotional challenges. A Canadian of African descent, Ope's work is informed by his rich cultural heritage and his deep well of empathetic understanding.

Ope is a skilled active listener, intuitive facilitator, and compassionate guide. His extensive training in therapeutic practices and his vast experience as a healthcare provider have honed his ability to offer innovative solutions and new perspectives to those facing a wide range of personal and emotional challenges. With his nonjudgmental and supportive approach, Ope has helped countless clients find their voice and gain the courage to pursue their goals and aspirations.

As an award-winning author of a book on self-discovery, Ope's words carry a transformative power that can soothe, challenge, and ultimately empower those he works with. In addition to his work as a healthcare provider and motivational coach, Ope is an avid reader, enjoys chess, and is a gifted facilitator. These diverse interests inform and enrich his unique perspective on life and the human condition.

Ope's dedication to his work is driven by a desire to help others, and he is committed to making a positive impact in the world. His wealth of cultural insight, deep knowledge, and keen perceptiveness make him a valuable resource for those seeking to improve their personal and professional lives.

Appendix:

Timeline of Key Events

- **1963:** Anthony Onyemaechi Elumelu was born in Jos, Nigeria, on March 22nd.

- **1985:** Tony graduates from Bendel State University (now known as Ambrose Alli University) with a Bachelor's degree in Economics.

- **1986:** Tony undertakes Nigeria's compulsory year of service in the National Youth Service Corps program.

- **1987:** He studies for a graduate degree—a Masters of Business Administration (MBA) degree from the University of Lagos.

- **1989:** Tony starts work at AllStates Trust Bank, rising through the ranks of the company.

- **1990:** He becomes the youngest branch manager in the country, aged 27.

- **1993:** Tony marries Dr. Awele Vivien.

- **1997:** Tony becomes the youngest CEO in Africa having acquired the struggling Crystal Bank and renamed it Standard Trust Bank (STB).

- **2005:** Tony makes history again with the merger of STB with United Bank for Africa (UBA) in a landmark move.

- **2005:** The new UBA Group is officially launched in August, becoming Nigeria's first mega-bank, with Tony as its chairman.

- **2010:** Tony leaves his position at UBA Group, creating the Tony Elumelu Foundation, which focuses on promoting entrepreneurship and economic development in Africa.

- **2010:** Tony also becomes the founder of Heirs Holdings (HH).

- **2011:** The principles of Africapitalism are devised by Tony.

- **2014:** He announces the creation of the Africapitalism Institute at the World Economic Forum event in Abuja.

- **2015:** Tony pledges $100 million over the next 10 years, aiming to support 10,000 entrepreneurs through the new Tony Elumelu Foundation Entrepreneurship Program.

- **2017:** He becomes the first African to win the Dwight D. Eisenhower Global Entrepreneurship Award in New York.

- **2018:** He joins the Board of Directors for the United Nations Global Compact.

- **2018:** The Foundation launches TEFConnect, the world's largest online platform for African entrepreneurs.

- **2020:** He is named in the TIME100 Most Influential People list.

- **2022:** TIME magazine recognizes Tony again in their inaugural TIME100 Impact list.

- **2022:** Tony signs a landmark agreement with the United Nations Capital Development Fund (UNCDP) in New York at the UN General Assembly.

- **2023:** Tony celebrates his 60th birthday.

References

A conversation with Tony Elumelu: 'The future of Africa truly belongs to the young ones but govts pay lip service to the importance, relevance and the future of our continent.' (2022, November 1). Time Africa Magazine. https://timeafricamagazine.com/a-conversation-with-tony-elumelu-the-future-of-africa-truly-belongs-to-the-young-ones-but-govts-pay-lip-service-to-the-importance-relevance-and-the-future-of-our-continent/

A mustard seed is planted: A history of UBA, pre & post-merger. (2019, September 4). UBA Group 57 Marina. https://www.ubagroup.com/57-marina/history-of-uba/

Abba, I. (2022, January 20). *What does Africapitalism actually mean?* The Republic. https://republic.com.ng/december-21-january-22/what-does-africapitalism-mean/

About the scheme. (2017). National Youth Service Corps. https://www.nysc.gov.ng/aboutscheme.html

Africapitalism and Africa's sustainable development. (2023, March 14). The Tony Elumelu Foundation. https://www.tonyelumelufoundation.org/africapitalism/africapitalism-and-africas-sustainable-development-the-tony-elumelu-foundations-contribution-to-the-sdgs

Areas and suburbs in Lagos: The best places to live in Lagos. (n.d.) Expat Arrivals. https://www.expatarrivals.com/africa/nigeria/lagos/areas-and-suburbs-lagos

Chukwuemeka, E. S. (2021, August 8). *History of education in Nigeria: True origin of education system in Nigeria.* BScholarly. https://bscholarly.com/history-of-education-in-nigeria/

Dizolele, M. P. (2022, May 12). *Tony Elumelu and why 'Africapitalism' works.* CSIS. [Podcast]. https://www.csis.org/podcasts/africa/tony-elumelu-and-why-africapitalism-works

Ebenofere. (2020). *15 popular Nigerian celebrities who were born and raised in Jos, Plateau State.* N Opera News. https://ng.opera.news/ng/en/entertainment/1ffec6f764d2dc7 1b3a41fa30aeea248

Elumelu emerges first African to receive the Dwight D. Eisenhower Global Entrepreneurship Award. (2017, December 6). Tony O. Elumelu.com. https://tonyelumelu.com/elumelu-emerges-first-african-to-receive-the-dwight-d-eisenhower-global-entrepreneurship-award

Elumelu, T. (2011). *Africapitalism The path to economic prosperity and social wealth: reinventing and rebranding Africa as a land of investment, innovation and entrepreneurship.* https://www.issuelab.org/resources/15291/15291.pdf

Elumelu, T. (2016, December 6). *Success is made up of 1% dreams and 99% hard work.* Tony O. Elemelu. https://tonyelumelu.com/success-is-made-up-of-1-dreams-and-99-hard-work

Elumelu, T. (2017a, December 3). *Letter to the next generation.* Tony Elumelu Foundation. https://www.tonyelumelufoundation.org/interviews-speeches/letter-to-the-next-generation-by-tony-o-elumelu-con

Elumelu, T. (2017b, December 5). *Tony Elumelu's speech in New York while receiving the BCIU Dwight D. Eisenhower Global Entrepreneurship Award.*

https://www.tonyelumelufoundation.org/interviews-speeches/speech-tony-elumelus-speech-in-new-york-while-receiving-the-bciu-dwight-d-eisenhower-global-entrepreneurship-award

Elumelu, T. (2019, January 2). *Years of spreading luck—everyone needs a little help.* The Cable. https://www.thecable.ng/years-of-spreading-luck-everyone-needs-a-little-help

Gibbs, N. (2016, April 2021). *How we pick the TIME 100.* TIME Magazine. https://time.com/4300131/how-editors-pick-the-time-100/

Jahan, S., and Mahmud, A. S. (n.d.) *What is Capitalism?* International Monetary Fund. https://www.imf.org/en/Publications/fandd/issues/Series/Back-to-Basics/Capitalism

Launch of the world's largest digital platform for African entrepreneurs, TEFConnect. (2018, October 30). The Tony Elumelu Foundation. https://www.tonyelumelufoundation.org/articles/the-launch-of-the-worlds-largest-digital-platform-for-african-entrepreneurs-tefconnect

McKenzie, D. (201o, September 10). *Restoring Nigeria's banking image.* CNN. http://edition.cnn.com/2010/WORLD/africa/09/10/tony.elumelu.nigeria/index.html

Obiora, C. (2021, December 3). *38 rare images of what Lagos looked like 50 years ago.* BuzzNigeria. https://buzznigeria.com/old-images-lagos/

Ogunleye, E. (1990). *The Phenomenal growth of the Nigeria banking industry in the 1980s and the Need for strategic planning in the 1990s.* CBN Bullion, 14(4), 36-39.

Okwumbu-Imafidon, R. (2022, January 22). *Tony Elumelu: From applying for a job he was not qualified for to owning a tier-1 bank.* Niarametrics. https://nairametrics.com/2022/01/22/tony-elumelu-from-applying-for-a-job-he-was-not-qualified-for-to-owning-a-tier-1-bank/

Our History. (n.d.-a) Heirs Holdings. https://www.heirsholdings.com/hh-at-ten

Our History. (n.d.-b) UBA | United Bank for Africa. https://www.ubagroup.com/nigeria/about-us/history/

Paul-Gindiri, M. (2018, May 27). *The Igbos were being killed. Biafran War Memories.* https://biafranwarmemories.com/2018/05/27/the-igbos-were-being-killed/

Popli, N. (2022, March 28). *Tony Elumelu tells the TIME100 Impact Awards Gala: The world is in need more than ever before.* TIME Magazine. https://time.com/6161497/tony-elumelu-time100-impact-awards-gala/

Spice, A. (2017, January 12). *Doing it in Lagos: How 80s Nigeria embraced funk and boogie.* The Vinyl Factory. https://thevinylfactory.com/features/doing-it-in-lagos-nigeria-soundway-boogie/

The History and Evolution of United Bank for Africa - Narrated by Group Chairman, Tony O. Elumelu. (2022, February 16). United Bank for Africa. [Video]. YouTube. https://www.youtube.com/watch?v=nv1AEbUDvVQ

The power of 1.8 Billion: Adolescents, youth, and the transformation of the future. (2014). The United Nations Population Fund. https://www.unfpa.org/sites/default/files/pub-pdf/EN-SWOP14-Report_FINAL-web.pdf

The 7 pillars of the TEF Entrepreneurship Programme. (n.d.). The Tony Elumelu Foundation. https://www.tonyelumelufoundation.org/tef-entrepreneurship-programme/7pillars

The Tony Elumelu Foundation launches Africapitalism Institute. (2014, May 18). The Tony Elumelu Foundation. https://www.tonyelumelufoundation.org/news/tony-elumelu-foundation-launches-africapitalism-institute

Tips for young professionals. (2022, August 11). Tony O. Elumelu.com. https://tonyelumelu.com/tips-for-young-professionals

Toast to Tony Elumelu at 60. (2023, March 25). Guardian Editor. The Guardian Nigeria. https://guardian.ng/saturday-magazine/toast-to-tony-elumelu-at-60/

Tony Elumelu attends the 77th UN General Assembly: Entrepreneurship, sustainability and partnerships. (2022, September 27). Heirs Holdings. https://www.heirsholdings.com/tony-elumelu-attends-the-77th-un-general-assembly-entrepreneurship-sustainability-and-partnerships

Tony Elemulu's wife, Dr Awele Vivien Elumelu, is a silent business magnate. (2021, June 3). Business Elites: Africa. https://businesselitesafrica.com/2021/06/03/tony-elumelus-wife-dr-awele-vivien-elumelu/

Trade growth to ease in 2011 but despite 2010 record surge, crisis hangover persists. (2011, April 7). World Trade Organization. https://www.wto.org/english/news_e/pres11_e/pr628_e.htm

UBA founder, Tony Elumelu, urges African leaders to better the continent. (2019, March 15). The Independent. https://www.independent.co.ug/uba-founder-tony-elumelu-urges-african-leaders-to-better-the-continent/

Ugochukwu, I. (2021, August 14). *Why South Africa needs to pay attention to its youth demography*. IOL. https://www.iol.co.za/business-report/opinion/why-south-africa-needs-to-pay-attention-to-its-youth-demography-0f1d4c4e-b428-52c0-88ba-ecfb7a7618c0

Wahab, B. (2018, January 4). *How 50 kobo increase in food caused nationwide students' protest.* Pulse Nigeria. https://www.pulse.ng/communities/student/ali-must-go-how-50-kobo-increase-in-food-caused-nationwide-students-protest/43tjyvp

Youth entrepreneurship and innovation multi-donor trust fund. (n.d.). African Development Bank Group. https://www.afdb.org/en/topics-and-sectors/initiatives-partnerships/jobs-for-youth-in-africa/the-youth-entrepreneurship-and-innovation-multi-donor-trust-fund

Image References

Annandale, R. (2016, September 23). *Man holding incandescent bulb* [Image]. Unsplash. https://unsplash.com/photos/7e2pe9wjL9M

Cocoparisienne. (2017, October 25). *Hands Cohesion Together* [Image]. Pixabay. https://pixabay.com/photos/hands-cohesion-together-people-2888625/

Freeman, R. (2021, February 8). *New Beginning – Exiting the Tor* [Image]. Unsplash. https://unsplash.com/photos/_J8IRsA4hG0

Jildén, A. (2014, January 29). *A look across the island* [Image]. Unsplash. https://unsplash.com/photos/yb0Qs65aZmc

Mars, B. (2019, March 15). *Man standing near high-rise building* [Image]. Unsplash. https://unsplash.com/photos/GzumspFznSE

Milkovic, T. (2018, March 11). *As days go by* [Image]. Unsplash. https://unsplash.com/photos/rMx6DPhGGrk

Nygård, A. (2021, July 25). *Person holding clear glass ball* [Image]. Unsplash. https://unsplash.com/photos/v5mEr9CfG18

Owolabi, S. (2019, November 13). *Danfo, a public means of transportation in Lasgo, Nigeria* [Image]. Unsplash. https://unsplash.com/photos/WSu7qcT3rVg

Spiske, M. (2021, April 10). *Daily newspaper economy stock market chart* [Image]. Unsplash. https://unsplash.com/photos/XrIfY_4cK1w

www.ingramcontent.com/pod-product-compliance
Lightning Source LLC
Chambersburg PA
CBHW072211290526
45794CB00004B/1722